SUCH IS LIFE!

A Close Encounter with Ecclesiastes

SUCH IS LIFE!

A Close Encounter with Ecclesiastes

Lloyd Geering

POLEBRIDGE PRESS
Salem, Oregon

This edition first published in 2009 by Steele Roberts Publishing Ltd. Postal Address: Box 9321. Wellington New Zealand.

Cover and interior design by Robaire Ream
Cover illustration by Robaire Ream

Library of Congress Cataloging-in-Publication Data

Geering, Lloyd, 1918-
 Such is life! : a close encounter with Ecclesiastes / Lloyd Geering.
     p. cm.
 Includes bibliographical references (p.   ) and index.
 ISBN 978-1-59815-023-0 (alk. paper)
 1. Bible. O.T. Ecclesiastes–Criticism, interpretation, etc. 2. Skepticism–Biblical teaching. 3. Imaginary conversations. I. Title.
 BS1475.52.G44 2010
 223'.806–dc22

                                           2010026790

to Tom Hall
in grateful acknowledgement of his encouragement and
helpful suggestions in my writing of this and earlier books

TABLE OF CONTENTS

PART ONE

Introduction

1

THE HERETICAL BOOK
OF THE BIBLE

Christians have long regarded the Bible as a holy book, and it was often referred to as the Word of God. People came to believe it was true in everything it said, free from all error—whether in theology (knowledge of God), ethics (knowledge of right and wrong), history (knowledge of the past) or science (knowledge of the world).

By the nineteenth century its "science" was disputed, and then its history of human origins. In the late twentieth century its ethics and even its theology were being questioned. There has recently been a burst of books containing damning criticisms of basic Christian beliefs—such as Richard Dawkins' *The God Delusion*, Christopher Hitchens' *God Is Not Great* and *The End of Faith* by Sam Harris. These sceptical and atheistic authors give the impression that they are pioneering a new path. They ignore that much of their scepticism was not only being expressed more than two thousand years ago but even found its way into the Bible itself.

Tucked away in the Bible we find one book that seems to question much that is in the rest. It is a book that most devout Bible readers rarely mention, that has been almost totally ignored by theologians, and whose teaching has never been referred to in any doctrinal statements of the church. Most Bible-lovers, should they accidentally stumble upon this book, will surely be surprised by what they read and likely feel embarrassed to find it in the Bible.

Yet the church has never tried to suppress this book, because the ancient Jews had already put their stamp of approval upon it by accepting it into the canon of the Hebrew Bible at the Council of Jamnia in 90 CE. Admittedly, that was only after considerable controversy between the opposing rabbinical schools of Hillel and Shammai, which represented the liberal and conservative wings of Jewish thought. Even then the reason given for its acceptance was not the validity of its religious ideas but the belief that it had been written by Solomon.

The ancient Church Fathers even thought they could find definite teachings about the Holy Trinity and the Atonement in this book. Some liberal scholars of today tend to treat Ecclesiastes as a schoolmaster leading people to Christ. It has even been claimed that he captures the futility and meaninglessness of life, when lived without God. The fallacy in this argument lies in the assumption that this book was specifically written to be included in a collection of holy writings; in fact, like most of the books in the Bible, it was originally intended to be read on its own.

Strangely enough this book bears a rather churchy kind of title, for it is commonly known as Ecclesiastes (Qoheleth in Hebrew), which means roughly "the preacher" or "the proclaimer." This is not a personal name but a role title. Yet this book completely undermines much of what is traditionally preached from Christian pulpits. Its message is quite impossible to reconcile with most of the rest of the Bible. Indeed, it openly questions the validity of the doctrine (held by all Jews, Christians and Muslims) that God rules this universe in a loving way that ensures justice for all. More than any other book in the canon, Ecclesiastes provides clear evidence that the Bible is a collection of books that are not only of human origin but reflect human thought and experience.

The Growth of the Bible

So how did Ecclesiastes ever come to be included in sacred scripture? To answer this question we must first go back to the origin and development of the Bible. The Bible did not fall from heaven, though fundamentalists often treat it as if it did. It was not sent directly by God through angels, as Muslims believe to have been the case with the Qur'an. The Bible did not even come through the mind of one man, as the Qur'an most probably came from the mind of Muhammad. The Bible, as its name from the Greek word *biblia* (books) tells us, is a *collection of books.*

Although it contains insights and wisdom that caused it to become highly valued, all the material in the Bible is human in origin. The assembling of the material into books and the collection of the books into the Holy Bible took place over a period of more than a thousand years.

The earliest material originated in oral tradition, the way all pre-literate societies transmitted cultural knowledge. Somewhere between the tenth to the eighth centuries BCE, portions of this accumulating oral tradition began to be transcribed into written form and collected on scrolls. Beginning no later than the fifth, and as far down as the second century BCE, whole sections and even complete books were actually composed in written form. These texts, by many different authors nearly all of whom are unknown, were then collected into groups and came to assume the status of Holy Scripture: the *Torah* (Law) by about 400 BCE, the *Prophets* by about 200 BCE and the *Writings* no later than the first century CE. That's why, according to the Gospels, Jesus knew the Jewish Bible as "The Law, the Prophets and the Writings."

Christians inherited all these from Judaism when they adopted as their own Holy Scripture the Greek translation of the Hebrew Scriptures, known as the Septuagint, which also contained Jewish books written in Greek that are not in the Hebrew Bible. These latter were all part of the Christian Bible until the Protestant Reformation. It was not until after such Christian writings as the letters of Paul and the four Gospels gradually came to be considered of significance equal to that of Jewish Holy Scripture that by the third century they were added to the Bible and named the New Testament. Thereupon, the writings inherited from Judaism, which until then had been "the Scriptures," became known as the Old Testament. (It would have better translated as the Old Covenant).

Even this much knowledge of how the Bible evolved begins to undermine the long-held notion that the Bible is quite different from all other books. It was not God who made the books of the Bible holy; it was the growing consensus of humans, first Jewish and then Christian, that gave them that status. The Bible is thus a library of books, and like any library it can claim neither to have a single author nor always to speak with the same voice. For that reason it often reflects the ignorance and even the prejudices of our ancient spiritual ancestors as well as their wisdom. Because most of the books were originally intended to be read independently of each other, they naturally reflect widely different and often conflicting viewpoints.

The Old Testament is best regarded as a cultural treasure. It preserves the traditions of ancient Israel expressed in a great variety of literary genres—myth, legend, history, prophetic oracle, song, poetry, drama and proverb. This variety points to the richness of the collection and helps to explain why Ecclesiastes found a place within it. Because the Bible has long been treated as one book (and authored by God to boot!) people have not only overlooked but often deliberately ignored the variety of ideas and beliefs it contains.

The dogmatic belief that it was to be regarded as the "word of God in written form" implied that it could not possibly contain any contradictory statements. Pious commentators went to absurd lengths to reconcile inconsistencies. From the time of the so-called heretic Marcion (d. *c* 160 CE), who, to his credit, saw that the Jewish Bible could not easily be reconciled with what Christians were then writing, the Old Testament came increasingly to be understood and interpreted through Christian eyes. Only since the advent of modern scholarship in the last two hundred years has the variety within the Bible been rediscovered and each tradition valued for its own sake.

Israel's Traditions

The traditions of ancient Israel developed along four parallel paths that were contemporaneous, even though their present place in the canon gives the impression they belonged to successive periods of history. Further, they continued to be clearly distinguishable even after they had been committed to writing.

For Jews the most authoritative stream of tradition is found in the first five books, known as the Torah or Books of Moses. This collection, regarded as the founding tradition of the people of Israel, mainly narrates the Hebrew exodus from Egyptian slavery and the giving of the Law on Mt Sinai. Genesis, its first book, serves as the introduction to the whole and contains early legendary stories and tribal sagas describing events from the time of "Creation" to the emergence of the patriarchs. The Torah became the focal point of the synagogue, an institution that developed from the Babylonian Exile onwards, i.e. after 586 BCE.

A second stream of Israelite tradition described how the monarchy emerged out of the primitive tribal structure, and then focused on the divine authorization of the dynasty founded by David. This material is embedded in Joshua, Judges, Samuel, Kings—books that later became known as the Former Prophets to distinguish this stream from that of (the great) Latter Prophets. The Kingdom tradition was thought to have been founded and nurtured by the early prophets Samuel and Nathan, and came to be regarded as foundational to the corporate well-being of Israel. Consequently, this tradition suffered a severe shock when the Davidic kingdom came to an end in 586 BCE with the disastrous Babylonian invasion. But even after the return from the Exile, Jews continued to hope for the restoration of the Davidic kingdom, a hope that became an important factor in the later rise of Christianity.

A third stream of tradition was the Prophetic. This originally consisted of oracles, short messages thought to have come directly from God. It was this fact that gave rise to the later conviction that the whole of Holy Scripture was to be regarded as the Word of God. The prophetic stream is found chiefly in Isaiah, Jeremiah, Ezekiel and the so-called Twelve Minor Prophets. Whereas the priests were concerned with the meticulous observance of the legal prescriptions of the Torah, the prophets were seen as God's spokespersons, whose divine inspirations led them to make striking pronouncements about current affairs and events of the near future. Thus the priests had their eyes on how the past should shape present behavior, while the prophets focused on the present, interpreting it in such a way as to throw light on the immediate future.

A fourth tradition, now referred to as the Wisdom stream, was neither priestly nor royalist nor prophetic. As exemplified by its earliest text, the Book of Proverbs, it arose initially out of the oral folklore in which ordinary people reflected on daily life and passed on their insights and maxims from generation to generation. Oddly enough, the writers of the Wisdom books showed no more than a passing interest in official religious beliefs and practices. As a result, this stream was very "this-worldly" in its concerns and almost mundane in its content. Today we would describe it as secular.

The Wisdom stream eventually produced its own specialists, known as the sages. Jeremiah, for example, spoke of "priest, sage and prophet" (Jeremiah 18:18) almost as if the three were of equal status. It has even been suggested by some modern scholars that the sages established schools in which the Wisdom tradition was taught, discussed and added to. At first the sages simply collected all the anonymous sayings being transmitted in oral tradition. That is how the Book of Proverbs came to exist. But later sages produced longer compositions of their own, mostly in verse.

The work of these sages is found chiefly in Proverbs, some of the Psalms, Job, Ecclesiastes, Ecclesiasticus (also called the Wisdom of ben Sirach) and the Wisdom of Solomon. The latter two were included in the early Christian scriptures, although they were composed so late that the Jewish Rabbis did not include them in the final canon of the Hebrew Bible. That is significant, for it shows that whereas the canonical limits of the Torah and the Prophets were complete at the time of Christian origins, the Wisdom stream was still growing, and indeed thriving.

From our vantage point, some two thousand years later, it is illuminating to observe how the four streams of ancient Israel's early traditions tended to become segregated from each other. Out of the cultural tradition of ancient Israel there evolved three quite independent religious communities—Judaism, Christianity and Islam—and in each of these communities one of the four former streams became dominant. In Judaism the Torah remained central. In Christianity it was the Davidic royalist tradition that initially dominated: Jesus was acclaimed as the Messiah (the anointed successor to David) before being given divine status (Son of God) as the King of Kings, reigning over the Kingdom of God. In Islam the prophetic tradition dominated with Muhammad being acclaimed as "The Prophet," the greatest and hence the last of the prophets.

And what happened to the Wisdom stream? It was the Cinderella of the ancient Israelite culture. As Judaism, Christianity and Islam became more identified with the supernatural and the other-worldly, there was less place for the this-worldly and humanist stream that we now call Wisdom. As a result, Jews and Christians paid less and less attention to the Wisdom books even though their own Bibles contained these texts, and at last the Wisdom stream became neglected and even rejected. Only in the modern secular world, with the decline of the sense of the supernatural that has long sustained traditional Judaism, Christianity and Islam, has the Wisdom stream, being more secular, come into its own.

The Wisdom Genre

Most material in the Wisdom stream was composed in verse. It used a mode of versification, now known as parallelism, that is unique to Hebrew poetry. This prosodic style not only gave to Wisdom material an appropriate dignity, but it made it much easier to commit to memory. It takes the form of couplets in which the second half of the verse confirms the first half, either by extending its meaning or by repeating it in one of a variety of ways. For example,

> A wise son makes a glad father,
> but a foolish son is a sorrow to his mother.

Thus the earliest expression of Jewish Wisdom came in the form of maxims. Their content was much like the proverbial sayings found in every culture, such as our "A stitch in time saves nine." The Jewish Proverbs offer observations about natural phenomena and frequently occurring human situations. They prescribe patterns of behavior to follow to live a harmonious, satisfying life, free of stress.

But often in Proverbs, and even more in Ecclesiasticus and the Wisdom of Solomon, we find not just isolated maxims but collections of couplets on a common theme. This shows that the sages were much more than collectors of popular folklore. They were also creative authors, moving on from anonymous proverbs to the composition of sustained reflections on various aspects of life. They explored and expounded what they called *hokhma* (Wisdom). Eventually Wisdom came to be conceived as an objective entity that played an active, personal role in human affairs, and it was always spoken of in the feminine gender. This means that Wisdom was being quite consciously personified. Later the Greek word for wisdom, *sophia* was given a role in Christian mythology as Saint Sophia. The great church erected about 550 CE by the Emperor Justinian in Constantinople (now Istanbul) was dedicated to her.

The Hebrew word for wisdom is frequently associated with words meaning "understanding" and "knowledge." It can refer to such things as political insight, knowledge of nature, discernment of right and wrong, and even technical skill. The sages, particularly in the earlier period, dealt mainly with the immediate issues of everyday life and rarely attempted to wrestle with ultimate questions. In their view, the world should be accepted just as it is. It was more important to discover and follow the rules of the game of life than to attempt to change the rules to suit yourself.

This worldly human wisdom was most commonly expressed in a form called a *mashal,* a term covering anything from one-liners to stories. Since the root meaning of the word is "to be like," *mashal* is more correctly translated as "parable," even though the English translations often render it as "proverb." Wisdom was thus frequently expressed in the form of comparisons or mini-parables such as:

> He who meddles in a quarrel not his own
> is like one who takes a passing dog by the ears.

The composition of these couplets eventually led to longer and more integrated works such as Job and Ecclesiastes. Job takes the form of a carefully constructed drama exploring the issue of why innocent people often suffer while the wicked go unpunished. Ecclesiastes, for its part, is the monologue of a man wrestling with the ultimate issues of life and finding no answers.

When we compare the Wisdom books with the other three streams of tradition in the Old Testament, the first thing that strikes us is the almost complete absence of such great themes as the destiny of Israel as a people, the Exodus Tradition, the Davidic dynasty and the prophetic expectation of divine intervention in the flow of history. It's not that the sages did not know about these themes, for they do occasionally reflect them. It is rather that they deemed these topics not sufficiently practical to be more than marginally related to the more pressing matters of daily life.

In short, the sages were not concerned with the destiny of the Israelite people as a whole. They focused on the daily life of the human individual. Moreover, they were interested not in Israelites alone, but in all humans. The Wisdom stream contains no reference to Israel as the chosen people and no hint of ethnic or racial superiority. The sages felt free to borrow from their counterparts in other cultures, especially Egyptian and Mesopotamian. For example, one chapter in Proverbs derives from a composition by an Egyptian writer. As the great Old Testament scholar Gerhard von Rad observed, "More than in any other intellectual sphere, Israel's Wisdom has borrowed from neighboring cultures."

The Wisdom stream was thus very cosmopolitan; today we would say it was ecumenical or global in its outreach. It was as if Christian clergy today felt free to place on the lectern alongside the Bible the *Meditations of Marcus Aurelius* and the *Rubaiyat of Omar Khayyam* and treat them as equally valid material for the Scripture lessons in church. The sages were concerned with what is universally human, and hence showed interest in all cultures.

Perhaps this is partly why the writers of the Wisdom tradition came to regard Solomon as their spiritual father. The reign of Solomon was marked by a free interchange of cultural resources along with its international trade. The fame of Solomon's kingdom is said to have become the talk of what was then the known world. The Queen of Sheba made her celebrated visit to inspect for herself the wealth and power of the famous king and to discover the secret of his wisdom. In the judgment of the sages, the splendor and wealth of the Solomonic kingdom resulted neither from divine favour nor from military conquest; they were due to Solomon's wisdom.

For this reason the Book of Proverbs was traditionally ascribed to him. The Wisdom of Solomon purports to come from him. The author of Ecclesiastes quite deliberately wrote as if he were Solomon. Jesus ben Sirach, who some time later wrote Ecclesiasticus, saw Solomon as the wise man *par excellence*. His mini-epic poem on the heroes of Israelite tradition starts with the well-known "Let us now praise famous men. . . ." There he wrote of Solomon:

How wise you became in your youth!
You overflowed like a river with understanding.
Your name reached to far-off lands,
and you were loved for your peace.
On account of your songs and proverbs and parables,
and because of your interpretations, all countries marvelled
at you.

The Wisdom tradition taught that all strife and conflict could be avoided if only people walked the path of wisdom. The sages believed humans should not look for help outside of themselves, expecting others to provide for them; rather, humans had it within themselves to achieve prosperity and peace and to make a success of life. The sages encouraged personal effort and individual initiative; people must be diligent and industrious. The sages took note of the busyness of all the other earthly creatures and were scathing in their denunciation of human slothfulness:

Go to the ant, O sluggard: Consider her ways and be wise.
Without needing orders from anyone,
she prepares her food in summer,
and gathers her sustenance in harvest.

Whereas the Torah, the Prophets and the Kingdom tradition were concerned with the destiny of Israel as a people, the Wisdom stream was concerned with the life of the individual person. Placing responsibility on the individual was the underlying theme and the great strength of the Wisdom stream; even the prophets eventually took it on board. This they did when Jeremiah and Ezekiel declared that, if a person committed a mortal sin, he alone should die for it; no person should be held responsible for the sins of another. They held up to criticism an ancient proverb which was consistently quoted in the land of Israel to explain undeserved suffering of innocent individuals: "The fathers have eaten sour grapes, and the children's teeth are set on edge." We do not find this proverb quoted in the Wisdom literature; no doubt the sages had already rejected it.

In the Wisdom literature the focus of attention was not on religious ritual, as it was in the books of Moses; it was on how humans lived their daily lives and on how to acquire the wisdom needed to deal adequately with the problems, enigmas and frustrations of life. So what is wisdom? Wisdom is the mental and emotional skill to respond most fruitfully to what life throws at us and to make the right choices.

But where is such sagacity to be found? It cannot be had for the asking, said the sages. It cannot be bought with gold and silver. Indeed even the earnest searcher will discover that it is hard to find. The best answer the sages could offer was contained in an oft-repeated line:

In reverence for the LORD is the beginning of wisdom.

This has often been interpreted to mean that to acquire wisdom we must worship God—in other words, if you like, go regularly to synagogue or church.

But that's not what the sages meant at all. They did not focus on God as the priests and prophets did—or as traditional Christians have done. Whenever they did introduce the name of God, which was not very often, they used it simply as if it were an accepted part of the cultural vocabulary, much as our Parliament opens its sessions with prayer to God. For the sages, "God" had become a symbolic term for the cosmic order. It symbolized all that humans must learn to accept about the way the world operates. It largely represented for them what William James termed "the unseen order of things," or what we today call "the laws of nature." This is shown by the fact that they sometimes used the word "God" as if it were a synonym for Fate, in the sense of "what will be will be!" For example, Jesus ben Sirach said, "Good things and bad, life and death, poverty and wealth, all come from the Lord."

Further, they referred to God in much the same way as we refer to "nature," and which we also commonly personify in the term Mother Nature. Moreover, unlike the priests and the prophets, the sages took a great interest in the natural world and frequently described it in an admiring and even reverent attitude. In the Book of Job, two whole chapters are devoted to describing nature's marvels.

So where the prophets and psalmists might have spoken about the attributes of God, the sages preferred to talk about the ways of Wisdom, speaking as if it were a personal entity and a feminine one at that. The many different metaphors the sages applied to Wisdom show that they were well aware they were using poetic imagery. In other words, they knew that in venerating Wisdom they were personifying the human capacity for making good decisions.

The sages spoke of Wisdom in much the same way as the Greeks spoke of the Logos or Reason. Wisdom had existed from the beginning of time, just as the Logos had. Just as the Fourth Gospel says "in the beginning the Logos was with God and the Logos was God," so the sages said that Wisdom emanated from God and was God. They spoke of it as "a breath of the power of God" and "a pure emanation of the glory of the Almighty."

The sages exhorted people to take full responsibility for their own lives and not to look to God to deliver them from evil by miraculous interventions in either nature or human history. In their encounter with the world, humans were on their own. Since most things in life could not be changed, people had to learn how to make the most of the choices that still lay open to them. The sages relegated God to the role of an impersonal creative force that had shaped the world to be as it was, that constituted the laws of nature, but that showed no interest in human affairs or destiny. Since nature could not be humanly manipulated, reverence for its structure was the beginning of wisdom.

Naturally, these convictions placed the sage in considerable tension with the other Israelite leaders, whether prophet, priest or royalist. This tension is not unlike that which occurred very much later between Erasmus, the Renaissance humanist and Luther, the Protestant champion of divine grace. It is the same tension—amounting at times to animosity—that exists today between secular humanists and fundamentalists. The latter, however, cannot rightly claim, as they often do, that they are simply being true to the Bible; for as we've just seen, this tension is clearly present in the Bible itself. The voices of the ancient sages can no longer be ignored or suppressed. From their place in the Bible they speak to our times in a remarkably relevant way.

The Book of Job

Out of the Wisdom stream there came an anonymous book that Alfred Lord Tennyson once referred to as the greatest poem ever written. We know it as the Book of Job, and it preceded Ecclesiastes by perhaps a century. The anonymous sage who wrote it mounted a dramatic challenge against what had become the standard Jewish answer to the problem of evil. The Book of Job is a courtroom drama in which Job charges God with being immoral for allowing the wicked to prosper and the righteous to suffer. The twentieth-century Nazi Holocaust of the Jewish people is the supreme modern example of the sort of events that perplexed and offended this sage.

Throughout this book the traditional solution to the problem of evil is expressed in a variety of ways through the mouths of Job's "comforters." But Job was having none of their pious pussyfooting, and challenged God to defend what he had done. The comforters naturally regarded this charge as blasphemy and self-righteous human hubris; and in the end, filled with disgust, they deserted him.

At last God answered Job out of the whirlwind with a long list of rhetorical questions that were intended to shame Job into acknowledging that he did not really know what he was talking about. This is, of course, the final put-down in any argument because it leaves nothing more to be said. So Jews and

Christians have traditionally interpreted the Book of Job as the moral vindication of God by God himself. God always has the last word and humans are in no position to challenge him. (Christian fundamentalists, and even such a great theologian as Karl Barth, may be judged to be the modern counterparts of Job's comforters.) But such a view forgets to ask who put these speeches into the mouth of God, as he spoke "out of the whirlwind." It was not God but a human author. Was this the same man as he who had initially raised the moral problem through the character Job? Or were the words added by a more devout voice, one who wanted to avoid any charge of blasphemy by effectively closing down the debate? That is not clear.

What we can say is that, in the Book of Job, an ancient sage pointed to a very serious moral problem present in the developing monotheism and left it unresolved. It began to surface again with the advent of modernity, sometimes referred to as humankind's "coming of age." The philosopher Leibniz (1646–1716) coined a special term for this moral problem associated with the traditional belief in God—*theodicy*. How can we reconcile the belief in an almighty and all-loving God with the phenomenon of cataclysmic evils that from time to time afflict humankind? Already in the eighteenth century the Lisbon earthquake of 1755 made it increasingly difficult to defend God's apparent indifference to innocent suffering. The Nazi Holocaust finally convinced many theologians, Jewish and Christian alike, that the personal God of theism was dead. As Rabbi Richard Rubenstein put it, "Even the existential leap of faith cannot resurrect this dead God after Auschwitz."

It is not too much to say that the sage who wrote the Book of Job drove the first nail into the coffin of the traditional God, even though it was not until the 19th and 20th centuries that this "God" finally expired, as Nietzsche so dramatically put it.

Moreover, starting with Job, the sages affirmed the complete mortality of the human condition; they did not regard departure to Sheol (the mythical underworld of the dead) as in any sense a "life after death." It was simply a euphemism for death.

The finiteness of human existence was best expressed by the greatest of all the sages in the pre-Christian era. We know him as Ecclesiastes.

The Book of Ecclesiastes

As we've noted earlier, Ecclesiastes is the Greek translation of the Hebrew *Qoheleth*, a word that means "the preacher." Qoheleth chose to write as if he were the re-incarnation of Solomon. He not only rejected the early Israelite beliefs that Job had already so brilliantly challenged, but he went so far as to hold up to critical enquiry the pursuit of wisdom itself. He conceded that the path of wisdom was more profitable than the way of folly, but observed that, in spite of this, death comes to the wise man just as it does to the fool.

Qoheleth shows himself more than a little disillusioned with human attempts to find permanent solutions to the problems of life. Two refrains keep appearing in his book. You may be familiar with the first of them, which has often been translated, "Vanity of vanities, everything is vanity!" That is not a good translation. The Hebrew word *hevel* he uses here refers to the breath that comes out of our mouths on a frosty morning. It soon disappears. So Ecclesiastes complains that wherever he turned, he could find nothing solid or permanent. Trying to create something lasting, he said, is as futile as chasing the wind. Everything eventually passes away and disappears. Another rendering of this lament would be, "Emptiness, emptiness, everything's empty."

Qoheleth developed what we today call an existentialist attitude toward life. He acknowledged that "God had made everything beautiful in its time" and had given human beings more than enough with which to occupy themselves. God had even created them in such a way that their minds can encompass (through the power of imagination) the whole universe of space and time. Yet the work of God remains hidden and can lead humans to adversity as readily as to prosperity. He finds that what happens to people in life is often unfair, and concludes that human existence is utterly devoid of any purpose. Things happen mostly by chance. Since life is like a trip to nowhere, we must forget about any desirable destination and simply enjoy the journey. These reflections kept leading our sage back to his second theme: the best thing we can do in life is to eat and drink and find enjoyment in what we do.

More than any priest, prophet or even sage before him, Qoheleth examined the nature of human existence. He asked some basic questions: What does it mean to be human? In the absence of any certainty or permanence, how can we get the best out of life? In doing so he raised the pursuit of wisdom to a higher level. True sages had to do more than collect gems of wisdom, select the best, and pass them on to their students. Wisdom is not an immutable body of knowledge, and it is vain to imagine that it is. We must personally walk the path of wisdom for ourselves rather than expect to receive it from others ready-made. So the role of the sage was not to provide instant wisdom for the foolish and unlearned; the words of the sage, says the Book of Ecclesiastes, were to be like a sharp goad forcing hearers to shake off their complacency and to pursue wisdom for themselves.

From this it is clear the words of Ecclesiastes should never be acclaimed as absolute truth. They are every bit as subject to critical examination as he himself was critical of what had gone before him. Besides, more than two thousand years separate us from their historical and societal context. We live in a very different culture and we have many different beliefs. But has the basic human condition changed all that much? We shall now try to find out, by engaging in conversation with Ecclesiastes.

2

ENGAGING WITH
ECCLESIASTES

Until about two hundred years ago the Bible was regarded by all in the Christian world as the repository of timeless truths. This implied that what the Bible contained was not only true for all time but could also be readily understood by people of all eras and cultures. The words of the Bible were thought to transcend the passing of time.

Such a conviction came under threat with the emergence of the modern world and our increasing awareness of the phenomenon of historical and cultural development. Languages manifest many of the attributes of life, but while they live and continue to be used as tools of communication, they keep changing in both vocabulary and in syntax. Only dead languages are static.

In living languages new words and concepts may arise at any time, flourish for a while, and then become obsolete or fall into disuse. Some words change their meaning quite significantly. For example, "I believe" used to mean "I put my trust in," but now it commonly means "it is my opinion that. . . ." No person in the sixteenth century would ever have dared say, "I believe in the Devil," yet I often hear conservative Christians say that now. It is because words change their meaning that many people today find it difficult to understand and appreciate Chaucer, or even Shakespeare.

Language originated as a medium of communication between humans, and an extraordinarily creative and powerful facility it has proved to be. Human language is the basis of human culture and, unless we are nurtured by other humans (and this normally means being shaped by one of the many language-based human cultures that exist), we do not advance from an essentially animal existence to a genuinely human one.

Since language is both powerful and creative, it is not at all surprising that whoever composed the first chapter of the Bible characterised it as the medium by which God created the world. God had only to utter the necessary words and each section of the world came into being immediately—by divine fiat, as we say. By the time the prologue of St. John's Gospel was being written, its author had virtually come to equate God with the spoken word by which he, like us, can reason, plan and design.

As I explain at greater length in my book *Tomorrow's God, How We Make Our Worlds*, it is only through the names, concepts, ideas and oral stories by which a living language expresses meaning that we create for ourselves a world. And when we make our various decisions in life, it is always to the world we have unconsciously constructed in our imaginations that we are making our response. Each of us is at the centre of our own world, and from that central point we survey the world as we have constructed it in our minds.

Whatever we think and say always remains relative to the world in which we see ourselves living. It is impossible for us to jump out of our cultural context and view reality from some neutral, timeless standpoint. It is impossible for us to attain to what we often refer to as "timeless truths" for the simple reason that our statements always remain contingent to our own time and place. Ironically, such a conclusion is wholly consistent with what Ecclesiastes repeatedly reminds us: nothing is permanent, nothing lasts forever.

This is something we too readily overlook when we read words written long ago and in a cultural context very different from our own. We tend quite unconsciously to understand all earlier writings against the background of our own time and culture. Those writings raised to the status of holy scripture— such as the Bible, the Qur'an, the Vedas, the Dhammapada, the Analects of Confucius—have long been treated as emanations from a timeless world that is equally relevant to all eras of human history. However much we may value the words of great teachers of the past, then, we must always remain aware that their words do not automatically and necessarily mean the same to us as they did to the people for whom they were first composed.

It can be challenging enough to translate from one living language into another, especially if they reflect very different cultures. The problem becomes greatly magnified when we move from antiquity into the modern world, because the breathtaking expansion of available knowledge has resulted in a radical change in many basic beliefs about ourselves and our world.

The Bible was written in three different languages over a period stretching from about 900 BCE to 150 CE. Once the Bible came to be treated as the timeless "word of God," people all too easily forgot that it was a set of ancient books. Although other writings from the same period are read today only by a few scholars, most Bible readers assume they should be able to read the Bible in the same way as they would a modern document. This problem has actually become even greater in the last two hundred years.

When the Bible was first translated into vernacular languages at the time of the Protestant Reformation, the world-view of the translators remained closer to that of the biblical authors than it is to ours. For them the sky above still visually represented the dwelling-place of God. Today we are aware of the vast universe of space and time that surrounds the tiny planet that is our earthly home. It is sometimes said, and justifiably so, that people in biblical times saw themselves living in a three-decker universe. It consisted of heaven above (God's domain in the sky), the flat earth below (inhabited by humans and all other earthly creatures), and the underworld (inhabited by the dead).

All of this and more has to be taken into account when attempting to read and understand the Bible; otherwise, in translating it we are in danger of unintentionally distorting what its authors intended to say. Not a little of what devout Christian readers and preachers thought they were finding in the Bible has resulted from subtle reinterpretation of what they read. For example, the Decalogue (Ten Commandments) is still commonly appealed to as the ultimate, and timeless authority on morals—even though a cursory examination shows it was originally addressed to a cultural situation very different from ours. The commandment to honour our parents is often assumed to provide the basis for the sound education of the young; but it was originally intended, among other things, to prohibit the practice of abandoning people to their death when they became elderly and infirm.

It is because of the difficulty I've been describing that it is so easy to read *into* the Bible what we want to find there. When Roman Catholic authorities expressed their fear of what would happen if the Bible were made available in the vernacular for all to read, they had a valid point. To understand and interpret these ancient books adequately, we first need to absorb a good deal of background knowledge. Over the last two centuries a vast amount of new knowledge about the ancient world has enabled us to understand the Bible in terms of its original cultural background. Failure to use this knowledge leads to much distorted interpretation, and allows people to use the Bible to provide divine authority for their own opinions.

But even awareness of the problem does not give us any automatic immunity from misinterpretation. I've had this constantly in mind while attempting to understand Ecclesiastes. My first task was to prepare a fresh translation of the Hebrew text. I claim no authoritative expertise in this respect, but I did teach Biblical Hebrew for sixteen years, first within the University of Queensland and then in the University of Otago.

By the time the Book of Ecclesiastes was written, Hebrew was no longer the daily vernacular of the Jewish people, but the language of their scholarship and worship—a rough analogy would be the role of Latin in medieval Europe in both church and academia. The cognate Semitic language of Aramaic had already become the vernacular of the Jewish people in the Holy Land and remained so until the time of Jesus of Nazareth. Not surprisingly, therefore, the Hebrew text of the Book of Ecclesiastes reflects Aramaic influence and contains an occasional Aramaic word.

As noted above, translation from one language to another always involves some degree of interpretation, particularly when such a great gulf in both time and culture separates the original author and the modern translator. Further, as with all the books of the Bible, the text has sometimes suffered in the transmission. Let me assure you, however, that I have resorted to textual emendations only where supported by broad scholarly consensus. To be sure, scholars disagree on many little details; but I offer no footnotes on these matters because this book is intended for the general reader rather than for specialists.

Because words in one language often do not have exact equivalents in another, and since English has a much more extensive vocabulary than ancient Hebrew, I have sometimes translated the same Hebrew word with a variety of English words, depending on the context in which it appears.

While I have tried to keep as close as possible to the Hebrew text (as comparison with any of the well-known translations will show) I have attempted to express what Ecclesiastes was saying in contemporary English idiom. For example, I have frequently translated the literal phrase "under the sun" as "in this world" or "on the face of the earth." I have also tried to preserve the balanced cadence of the Hebrew poetry in which most of the book was written. I have omitted all the verse and chapter numbers; these later additions constitute an unwelcome intrusion into the thinking of Ecclesiastes, and in any case were not inserted into the standard Hebrew text until many centuries after the book was written.

The format I have chosen for discussing the content of the Book of Ecclesiastes is that of a series of dialogues between the author and me—a strategy to which the book readily lends itself because it consists not of a carefully organized forensic argument on the part of the author, but of a collection of relatively short observations that are not arranged in any particular order. Indeed, the epilogue to the book speaks of it as "the collected sayings." Therefore, when addressing questions to Ecclesiastes, I have felt free to draw his answers from any part of his book.

While I hope this device will make the discussion of the thoughts of Ecclesiastes more accessible and interesting for today's reader, it is important to acknowledge the problems it raises. Of course, it is as clear to me as it is to you that it is quite unrealistic for me to have a real dialogue with Ecclesiastes—and not only for the obvious reason that he has been dead for over two thousand years. Normally, when two people converse, they share both a common language and a common body of knowledge on which they draw in the course of their dialogue. Even then serious misunderstandings can arise. When two people have enormous differences in general knowledge and presuppositions, genuine dialogue becomes impossible, as it so often does, for example, between fundamentalist and progressive Christians.

Ecclesiastes thought and wrote in a language that lacked the versatility and extensive vocabulary of most modern languages, but an even greater challenge to establishing a meaningful exchange of ideas is posed by the explosion of knowledge in the past several centuries. Although Ecclesiastes is clearly more inclined to empirical than to speculative thinking, his experience was utterly devoid of such modern fields of knowledge as the physical and social sciences and the humanities. Indeed a reasonably bright ten year old of today has a grasp of the phenomenal world immeasurably greater than that of our ancient sage.

To enter into the spirit of the dialogue, therefore, you will have to undertake what Coleridge called a "willing suspension of disbelief" and suppose that Ecclesiastes has had the benefit of a brief but sufficiently wide-ranging introduction to our world that he can understand the points that this modern interlocutor is attempting to make and the questions to which he seeks answers. Surely a whirlwind acculturation course of a month or two would suffice to brief so observant and profound a thinker as Ecclesiastes on our brave new world and enable him to apply his wisdom to the issues that confront us today.

These dialogues are of necessity very one-sided, for Ecclesiastes has only very limited opportunity to question me or to elaborate and defend what he said so long ago. Therefore, when I draw attention to historical facts and persons that Ecclesiastes would not have been aware of, it is primarily for the benefit of the reader. I shall occasionally refer to historical figures who lived before Ecclesiastes, and it is possible he knew of some of them even though his words do not betray any evidence of this. But more commonly I shall briefly inform him about historical people and events of which he could not have had any knowledge because they came from later times.

One such person is Jesus of Nazareth. As a result of the research undertaken by the Fellows of the Westar Institute (a group of biblical experts commonly known as the Jesus Seminar) it now appears that once we strip away from the historical Jesus the mantle of supernatural divinity with which later tradition clothed him, the recoverable outlines of the human figure who emerges show him to be more of a sage than a prophet, priest, or king. This means that Jesus belongs to the Wisdom stream of Jewish tradition, and therefore a greater affinity exists between Ecclesiastes and Jesus than has generally been recognized. I have already drawn attention to this in my book, *Christianity without God*.

Unfortunately, we are so used to reading the highly developed portraits of Jesus in the Gospels that even when we isolate his most likely authentic words, we still tend to read them in the light of those later doctrinal developments. Thus we miss many points of similarity between Ecclesiastes and Jesus that can still be discerned. In my dialogues with Ecclesiastes I draw attention to both what he has in common with Jesus and where the two significantly differ.

Ecclesiastes, as we shall see, argued that the best thing we can do in life is to eat and drink and enjoy what we do. We are told in the Gospels that Jesus so thoroughly enjoyed food, wine and good company that his enemies accused him of being "a glutton and a drunk and crony of toll collectors and sinners." That shows that Jesus often exhibited a carefree spirit. His advice was,

> Don't fret about your life—what you're going to eat and
> drink, or about your body—what you're going to wear.
> There is more to living than food and clothing, isn't there?
> Take a look at the birds of the sky: they don't plant or har-
> vest, or gather into barns. Yet your heavenly Father feeds
> them. You're worth more than they, aren't you? Can any
> of you add one hour to life by fretting about it? Why worry
> about clothes? Notice how the wild lilies grow: they don't
> slave and they never spin. Yet let me tell you, even Solomon
> at the height of his glory was never decked out like one of
> them. If God dresses up the grass in the field, which is here
> today and tomorrow is thrown into the oven, won't God care
> for you even more, you who don't take anything for granted?

In short, Jesus not only enjoyed life as Ecclesiastes commended, but encouraged others to do the same. This is implied in such sayings as, "Leave it to the dead to bury their own dead." The difference between the two sages is not so much in the way they understood the nature of human existence, as in what they considered the best attitude to take towards it. In this respect it may be said that for Ecclesiastes the proverbial glass was half empty but for Jesus it was half full.

Strange as it may seem, I have found it in some respects easier to construct a series of dialogues with Ecclesiastes than it would be to do the same with Jesus. But there is a good reason for this: Ecclesiastes left his words behind in written form, and it is all we know of him. But since Jesus wrote nothing, our only access to his teaching is through the Gospels, where his authentic words have not only been translated into the non-Semitic Greek language (which was unfamiliar to most of those he taught and at best a second tongue to him), but they have become all but inextricably mixed up with words of a different genre that the evolving Christian tradition placed in his mouth. The great majority of liberal scholars now think we come closest to the original teaching of Jesus in his parables and aphorisms and in the so-called Sermon on the Mount. I shall draw on that material in the following dialogues.

The contribution of Ecclesiastes to the dialogues is printed in **bold italic** type. To make the exchanges as lively and realistic as possible under these extraordinarily strange circumstances I have taken the liberty of inventing some of the sage's responses but these will always be clearly distinguishable from his actual words by being printed in *italic*. Much of what is thus placed in the mouth of Ecclesiastes consists of connecting words and phrases to help the dialogue flow more smoothly, but occasionally I have gone further. As I proceeded, the realization suddenly came to me that this was similar to what the author of St. John's Gospel was doing when he created so many of the words he put into the mouth of Jesus. Indeed, my inventions are considerably less substantive than his, for they are always consistent with what Ecclesiastes actually wrote, whereas the Jesus of St. John turned out to be very different from the Jesus of the other three Gospels.

Some readers may legitimately complain that I have manipulated the text of the biblical Book of Ecclesiastes to have him saying things he neither said nor intended to say. Up to a point that is true, though I have tried never to distort the words left behind by Ecclesiastes. Rather, I have attempted to bring Ecclesiastes to life in our day by enabling him to utter words as relevant to our time as his were to his own, and thus to bridge the many centuries that divide us from him. By immersing myself in his words over the last two years I have often experienced the quite unexpected sensation of conversing with a live person. And I must say that I found his thinking very congenial, though by no means did I always agree with him.

This enterprise has been both challenging and rewarding. In particular, it has brought home to me in a striking way how often we unconsciously read ancient texts such as the Bible, the Qur'an and the ancient Greek philosophers against the background of our own cultural setting, instead of that in which the words were originally composed. I can only hope that readers will find themselves similarly challenged—and rewarded.

PART TWO

The dialogues

3

ECCLESIASTES,
WHO ARE YOU?

Hello! Is there anyone there? All I can hear at the moment is the low rumble of many voices. They remind me of the scene at the legendary Tower of Babel and make me wonder if I've travelled too far back in time.

Who are you?

I'm a voice from two millennia into your future and I'm attempting to send a message back into your times.

How is it we can hear you speaking to us from a time so far away into our future?

It's by means of an electronic device invented by our science fiction. We have many modern inventions that you people of ancient times would regard as impossible. By means of television we can hear and see people on the other side of the world. We have telescopes by which we can see what happened out in space millions of years ago. This device combines a bit of each and sends our voices back into the past.

But what do you expect to achieve by sending your voice back to us?

I'm hoping to make contact with a man we call Ecclesiastes.

There is no man of that name here.

How stupid of me! Of course you wouldn't recognize him by that name. That's the Greek translation of the pseudonym he chose for himself. He referred to himself by the Hebrew word

Qoheleth, that I have translated into English as "Proclaimer."
I don't know his real name.

We doubt if he wants to be disturbed in this fantastic manner,
so why do you seek him?

I've long been fascinated by what he wrote and would greatly
appreciate an opportunity to talk with him. I know this will
not be easy. Not only will I have to translate his words into the
English language of my day, but also I know that there was no
equivalent in your language for many of the ideas and concepts
that are widely understood in our world today.

How then could he possibly understand you?

As we go along I shall try to give him a brief explanation of the
new concepts that will be unfamiliar to him. I suspect that one
of the chief problems we shall face arises from the fact that
back then you viewed the universe we humans live in very differently from the way most of us in the twenty-first century do.
Without wishing to offend you biblical people in any way, let me
say that we sometimes speak of you as "flat-earthers."

But isn't it perfectly obvious to all sensible people that the earth
we live on is a largely flat surface that is "under the sun"? So
what's so odd about that?

I know it seems more or less flat, but ever since Galileo, a scientist of some four hundred years ago, we humans have come to
recognize that the surface of earth is not flat, but spherical. The
earth is a planet that revolves round the sun. That's why I translate your phrase "under the sun" as "on the face of the earth."

Further, all the heavenly bodies are made of the same basic
materials as the planet earth on which we live. In short, since
your era what people commonly think of as "the world" has
become magnified into an unbelievably vast universe.

Voice from the future, excuse my interrupting this conversa-
tion you are having with my friends here, but I think I am the
person you are looking for. It was indeed I who took the title

Qoheleth, that you say can be translated into other languages
as Proclaimer and Ecclesiastes.

Ecclesiastes—if I may so address you—how delighted I am
to hear your voice! Even though we cannot see each other,
at least we can hear each other and enter into some kind of
conversation. As I said earlier to your friends, I have long been
fascinated by the little book you wrote. In spite of the great
changes that have taken place in the world since you expressed
your thoughts—about twenty-three centuries ago by my reckon-
ing—some of them sound as if they are particularly relevant to
the world we live in today.

We like to think of ourselves as inhabitants of a global,
secular world, and members of a culture uniquely inclined to
analyse and challenge received truths, but I find that more than
two millennia ago you were asking questions and raising issues
that we are debating today! So I'm keen to talk to the person
who lies behind the "Proclaimer"? Can you tell me more about
yourself?

I, the Proclaimer, used to be the king over Israel in Jerusalem.

You seem to imply that when you wrote you were not the king.
Since no Israelite king ever abdicated, it is becoming clear to
me that you were not really the king but someone who wished
to remain anonymous by hiding your identity behind a pseudonym. Is it the case that the most I can ever learn about you as
a person is what I can deduce from the clues you've left behind
in your observations?

That's correct! I shall be interested to hear what clues you have
found.

The most obvious clue is that you wrote in Hebrew. That's the
language that remained peculiar to the Jewish people and was
preserved by them for religious purposes long after it had been
superseded by other languages for everyday use. This strongly
points to your being a Jew.

Secondly, since you attribute your words to someone who was once a king in Jerusalem, I conclude that you are well acquainted with the Jewish tradition and that you still identify with it. It's important for me to know that. Indeed, I had begun to have my doubts about your Jewishness, because there is such a complete absence in your book of what I would expect in one written by a Jew. You make no mention of Moses and the Torah, no reference to the prophets, and not so much as an allusion to Yahweh the God of Israel, and the promises he is reported to have made to his chosen people.

Don't you have a rather narrow view of what it means to be Jewish?

Perhaps I have. I suppose I've been assuming that back in your times there already existed the kind of Judaism that we associate with Jews today. I now recall learning that rabbinical Judaism did not assume its standard form until the second century of the Christian era. Before the Christian era you Jewish people were becoming quite diverse in your beliefs.

We were indeed. In addition to the priests there had long been the prophets. They were often very critical of the priests and said so in no uncertain terms. And then there were the sages, as Jeremiah acknowledged long ago. They by no means thought as the prophets did. Moreover, when our people became increasingly dispersed after the destruction of Jerusalem by the Babylonians, they encountered many new ideas, not only in Babylon, to which many were exiled, but also in other countries where they took refuge. The future our people faced was a highly uncertain one. Not surprisingly, there was much bewilderment and great diversity among us. Not all of us were happy with the way Ezra, from a century before my time, attempted to turn us into an exclusive people, separate from all others.

Your words certainly reflect that period of diversity and cultural change. Indeed they are so different from most other Jewish writings that I find it very surprising that your little book ever came to be accepted into what we've long known as the Bible.

What is the Bible?

It's a collection of Jewish and Christian writings treated as sacred because they were thought to have been divinely inspired. There is so much in your book that seems to be in conflict with the major themes and affirmations in the Bible that we could justifiably call you the biblical heretic. But of course when you wrote it, the Bible as we know it did not yet exist, and so you had no idea that your thoughts would eventually be included in it.

But where were you when you wrote it? That's what I would like to find out. Were you in Babylon or in Jerusalem? Perhaps it was even in Alexandria, the new Greek city founded in Egypt by Alexander the Great.

Didn't I make it clear in the title I gave to my book? **The Words of the Proclaimer, son of David, king in Jerusalem.** *Obviously I lived in Jerusalem.*

But that was the home of the Proclaimer, the pseudonym under which you chose to write. I'm trying to find out about the person behind the mask, and that's just what you seem reluctant to tell me. Further, since you insist on hiding behind your chosen persona, I don't know exactly *when* you lived. I strongly suspect from the kind of Hebrew you speak that it was after the Greeks had assumed the rule of the East, and I'm inclined to think that you were influenced by the Greek culture that was then spreading throughout the Mediterranean world.

Seeing you are reluctant to tell me about yourself, let me ask you about the role you chose for yourself. You refer to the author as "the son of David." I assume that you intended your readers to regard your words as coming from Solomon, even though you never mention him by name. Is that not so?

You can be the judge of that when you hear what I say:
I did things on a grand scale.
I built myself mansions and I planted myself vineyards.
I laid out for myself gardens and parks
and planted in them every kind of fruit tree.

I made myself reservoirs of water
to irrigate the orchard then sprouting with trees.
I acquired for myself slaves and servant-girls
even though I already had a large household
and already possessed cattle, sheep and goats,
more numerous than all my Jerusalem forbears had owned.
I amassed for myself such treasures of silver and gold
as only kings and nations can boast.
I acquired men and women singers,
and what delights all men most—mistresses galore!
And so I grew great, surpassing all who lived before me
in Jerusalem.

That sounds like Solomon all right—particularly the "mistresses galore." I suspect that even in your day you were still lamenting the loss of the kingdom of Judah, that had been established by David some seven hundred years before. Perhaps that's why you've apparently ignored the Exodus tradition of Moses (at least you never mention it) and, instead, evoked the great days of Solomon in all his glory. Your decision to assume the persona of Solomon suggests to me that you hold the Davidic dynasty in high honour.

I do indeed! **Obey what the king commands, I say, on account of your oath of allegiance. Be in no hurry to leave the king's presence, nor persist in a cause that displeases him, for he can do whatever he likes. Since a king's word is final, who can say to him, "What are you doing?" Whoever obeys his command will experience no harm at all.**

Excuse me for saying so, Ecclesiastes, but I think that here I've caught you out. In answering my question you seem to have stepped aside from your persona and given me your own view on the subject of royalty, one that even contains a touch of cynicism.

So clearly you had a much more important reason than royal authority for putting your words into the mouth of Solomon: his reign was famous not only for its economic prosperity but for the cultural flowering to which it gave rise. Jerusalem became quite an international centre, where humanly based wisdom from around the world became so famous that the name of Solomon came to symbolise the epitome of wisdom. It was rather like the way the values that shaped English-speaking society in the nineteenth century became known as Victorian, after the reigning Queen Victoria of England.

So now I put it to you, Ecclesiastes: was it because of his reputation for wisdom that you identified with Solomon?

Yes indeed. That's why I said, **"Look! I've greatly increased in wisdom; I've surpassed all who lived in Jerusalem before me. My mind has absorbed a vast amount of wisdom and knowledge."**

Well then, since Solomon came to be honoured in Jewish tradition as the wise man par excellence, I imagine you'd have agreed wholeheartedly with Jesus ben Sirach, a Jewish sage who followed you by a century or two and addressed Solomon posthumously in these words:

> Your name reached to far-off lands,
> and you were loved for your peace.
> For your songs and proverbs and parables,
> and for your interpretations, the countries marvelled at you.

I agree with that whole heartedly, and wish I had written those words myself. You'll know of course that the Book of Proverbs was attributed to him. I've read it often.

I'm glad to have your confirmation as to why you adopted the persona of Solomon. Perhaps you could tell me why you think the words of the sages were so different in character from the oracles of the prophets.

The sages were chiefly concerned with the practicalities of daily living. To this end they were open to ideas and valuable insights they learned from other cultures as well as their own. The Wisdom tradition was found in Egypt and Babylonia

just as much as in our Jewish culture. The sages looked at life
from a human point of view and were little concerned with the
cultural and ethnic distinctions that separated the nations one
from another.

What you've just described we now call humanism. Indeed we
often refer to your Wisdom tradition as Hebrew humanism.
This, in turn, helps to explain why your reflections sound to us
so modern. It's only in the last century or so that humanism has
begun to flourish in the modern world.

But now let me sum up our conversation thus far. Though I
still know very little about your personal life, I'm now sure that
you were a Jew who, in the uncertain times you lived through,
felt more attracted to the Wisdom tradition than to the priestly,
prophetic and messianic traditions reflected in the Jewish people of your day. And from this distance in time we can say with
total assurance that you made a very significant contribution to
the Wisdom stream of Jewish tradition.

It is gratifying to hear you say so, but it greatly surprises me
to learn that my words are still being read in your day. I never
expected them to last as long as that.

Perhaps you underestimated yourself. Let's now see if that was
the case, for I'd like to turn to the content of your observations. As a sage you naturally pondered deeply on the nature
of human existence and, rather more than your predecessors,
you began to enunciate a personal philosophy of life. Can you
express that to me in a single word or phrase?

You want it in one word? Well, here it is. **Hevel! Hevel!**
Everything is hevel!

To be sure, you used but a *single* word, as I asked you to. It is the
very word with which you chose to start your book and which
you repeated from time to time as a kind of refrain. But I need
to pause before translating it, because it's a word for which
we have no exact English equivalent. The early English Bibles

rendered it as "vanity"; and accordingly many readers are familiar with your lament as: "Vanity of vanities! All is vanity!"

Unfortunately, the Hebrew word you use, *hevel*, does not really mean what is now conveyed by our word "vanity." Rather it denotes something like "mist" or "water vapour." In fact, it refers to the breath that comes out of the mouth on a frosty morning and just as quickly disappears into thin air before our very eyes.

And because you clearly use it metaphorically, we may need to use a variety of words to bring out more accurately what you intended in the various contexts in which you use it. Sometimes you use it to deplore how "short-lived" and "fast-fleeting" you find human life to be. Here you are using it to draw attention to how futile you judge all human endeavour to be. Do I understand you correctly?

Yes, indeed; whatever else it may be, life is short and nothing that we achieve lasts for long: "Fast-fleeting." "Impermanent." "Everything dissolves into nothingness."

Your proclamation of the impermanence of everything sounds rather Buddhist to me. But though the Buddha lived about two hundred years before you, I think it unlikely that you were familiar with his teaching, and therefore this theme of impermanence must be a strikingly original insight of your own.

As I said, it is one that makes you sound very modern. More than two millennia later many of us are only now coming to recognize that most of the physical world that we normally take to be eternal and unchanging is not so permanent after all. Our geologists tell us that mountains, valleys and whole continents are in a continual state of flux because of the movement of massive tectonic plates that move across the surface of the planet.

Further, ever since Charles Darwin wrote his book *On the Origin of Species*, our biologists have been telling us that the great variety of living species are not, as we long thought, fixed or permanent. Rather they have all evolved from earlier and now extinct species over very long periods of time. Moreover, our physicists tell us that the minuscule atoms that constitute matter are themselves composed largely of empty space, and can in turn be divided into particles and forces even less substantial. Indeed, rather like your *hevel*, matter itself can seem to disappear into thin air.

Of course that is all new to me. Yet I'm not wholly surprised to hear it, for it simply serves to confirm my thoughts about the world and my dismay at the impermanence of everything I observed.

How is it, then, that you were so far ahead of us in discovering the impermanence of everything? What was it that led you to this conclusion?

The way I put it, as you surely recall, was this: **I studied all human activities—everything that happens to people on the face of the earth.** *In doing so, I was struck by the ceaseless change that went on, and simply reported what I saw.*

Do you mean to say, then, that in the course of this study you never imagined that any of your insights came from some supernatural source? Your own prophets, for example, talked about hearing the word of God coming to them. And long after your era, Christians and Muslims claimed that some of their knowledge about the world had come to them by divine revelation.

No, I relied on no other sources, human or divine. As I said, **all this I saw for myself as I applied my mind to everything done on the face of the earth.**

That means you reached your conclusions on the basis of the evidence of your own senses. Today we call knowledge derived from our own direct and repeated experience "empirical." Empiricism is actually the basis of modern science, a widespread enterprise that began to develop in the Western world only after the sixteenth century, nearly two millennia after your day! Until then, people's knowledge had come almost exclusively from the cultural traditions into which they were born, and it was not thought wise to question it. "Thinking outside the box," as we now say, was strongly discouraged and sometimes even severely punished.

The few brave souls who did so in the eighteenth century were condemned as "freethinkers," but since that time more and more of us have been claiming the freedom to think for ourselves. Indeed modern educational methods encourage people to be independent in their thinking. Even though you lived in the ancient world, it seems to me that you could well be regarded as an empiricist and a freethinker.

Good gracious, I did not know I was such a dangerous fellow! First you tell me I'm a biblical heretic and now that I'm a freethinker.

Indeed you are. But claiming the right to think for ourselves does not ensure that the conclusions we reach are necessarily valid, for our attempts to express what we believe to be true cannot avoid having a strong subjective component. Since our beliefs always reflect the culture that shaped us, even those we arrive at on the basis of personal experience are affected by the limited nature of that experience. When our cultural horizons widen to include more knowledge, we may be forced to change our minds concerning what we believe to be true. That's why our beliefs can change considerably, even during the course of our own lifetimes.

*Naturally I agree with that for, as I said, **everything is impermanent, even our beliefs.***

But that means that we must be wary of making any absolute claims for our beliefs, especially since they are the basis on which we proceed to make our decisions about what is right and wrong behaviour. All this applies to you too.

Quite so; that's why I emphasised that I reached these conclusions only after a lifetime of reflection. And you'll recall *something else I said—**no human on earth is always in the right, and does only what is good and never goes wrong.***

I'm glad to hear you say so, for it reassures me that even though you express your conclusions quite strongly, you're ready to reconsider them in the light of new evidence that you've seen with your own eyes, or of new understandings you may arrive at. Perhaps as we go along you may even venture a new thought or two in the light of such evidence as I can present to you. But let's return to your chosen field of study—human behaviour and the phenomena of the natural world around you. How did you go about studying these?

*My passion for study arose from curiosity: wishing to know the why of things, **I devoted myself to research—to the rational understanding of everything that happens on the face of the earth.** For only by close observation can we hope to learn about causes and effects and thus describe events accurately.*

That sounds very modern indeed. In our day a phenomenal amount of research is being carried out in many different fields of human knowledge. It's because of research that the sum total of reliable knowledge now available to us has for some decades been expanding exponentially.

But though we moderns have access to this phenomenal body of knowledge, we cannot claim, as you do, that we've tested it with our own eyes; rather we have to trust the scientists who have done the empirical testing. To some extent, there-fore, we are seeing and understanding the universe through their eyes and minds.

Since you were relying on your own observations of "every-thing that happens on the face of the earth," let me ask you what in particular it was that you noticed.

*I noticed patterns in events. Let me put it this way: **The sun rises and the sun sets, and then it wearily returns to its place to rise once more. The wind blows to the south, and then turns to the north; it goes round and round and turns full*** *circle. All the rivers flow into the sea, yet the sea never over-flows. Back to the place from which they arose, the rivers return to flow once more.*

I see. You observed that natural phenomena keep repeating themselves; day follows day, month follows month, year follows year and "one generation passes away and another takes its place." It seems to me, then, that by fastening on these continuing regularities in nature, you came to recognize the considerable degree of order that exists in nature, observable patterns that were destined to become the foundation of what we call the laws of nature. Across the sea in Greece, about a century before you, a deep thinker called Aristotle had expounded a very detailed philosophy of nature. Had you ever heard of him?

No, his name is not known to me.

I thought not, as your book shows no hint of his influence. Nevertheless, it's clear that you were beginning to speculate about nature and I'm pleased to be able to tell you that it was that kind of intellectual exercise from which eventually arose the whole enterprise of empirical science. Indeed, until only a hundred years ago physics—the study of the physical world—was known as Natural Philosophy and psychology as Mental Philosophy.

But in observing that natural events repeat themselves in apparently endless cycles, you stumbled upon things that appeared to be permanent after all, even though you started off by deploring how impermanent you found everything to be. You discovered the existence of certain constants in the physical world. Could it be that despite your earlier and entirely justifiable complaint about the impermanence of everything, you found this encouraging?

Not at all, for the repetition that suggests permanence can become oppressive, and the endlessness of it daunting. As I said, all things become wearisome: there's more to be said than a

*man can utter, more to be seen than the eye can see, more to
be heard than the ear can hear.*

To some degree I can understand how your philosophising
brought you frustration, for there is no limit to the knowledge
that *can* be uncovered. That's clearly much truer in our day
than it was in yours. The modern world has witnessed a knowledge explosion so great that our minds are too small to master
more than a tiny portion of what is now available. Yet we find
the attainment of new knowledge can be very exciting. Why did
you not feel that also?

*But is all new knowledge really new? What I see is an end-
less succession of events that goes round in cycles. Indeed, the
conclusion I came to was this:* **Whatever has once existed will
exist again and past events will occur again, for there is nothing new on the face of the earth.**

I'm a little surprised to hear you say that. On the one hand
you complain that nothing lasts forever, and on the other you
lament that you find "nothing new on the face of the earth." I
detect an element of inconsistency here. I concede, of course,
that most if not all of us sometimes find life monotonous and
boring. In today's world we express these feelings in such expressions as "the daily grind" and "Monday-itis." And I must
concede that modern economists see the stock market moving
in cycles and our historians warn that if we do not learn the
lessons of history we are doomed to repeat them. But does that
really mean there is nothing new in this world?

*Just take anything of which people say "Look at that! It's
new!" Well, it already existed ages ago, but long before our
time. There is no longer any memory of the ancient times, just
as future events will be forgotten by those who come later.*

Well, your last point may be true enough, for indeed many happenings soon get lost in the quick passage of time; but that does
not mean that nothing is new. You appear to have jumped to

this conclusion from your observation that everything seems to go round in cycles, and therefore that anything that appears to be new must have occurred before, even if that occurrence has been long since forgotten. I suspect that in your day cultural change was so slow that it was rare for anything truly new to arise in the course of a person's lifetime.

With us, however, it's very different, and it's been so for a century or more. Indeed, in modern times we encounter so much novelty that we often find it difficult to deal with the degree of change to which we are subjected. I could give a long list, but for now let me mention only such everyday things as electricity, radio, television, computers, nuclear energy and cell-phones, to say nothing of such wonders as modern miracle medicines, organ transplants, aeroplanes and space travel.

I've no idea what you are talking about. Can you explain?

I would like to but it would take a very long time. I simply mention them to convince you that many new things have been created since your day. Moreover, the new sciences of astronomy and geology have brought us such detailed knowledge of the planet we inhabit and the vast universe that surrounds us that you'd be absolutely astounded by it all. In addition, through the sciences of anthropology and archaeology we've learned about the evolution of the human species that took place hundreds of thousands of years before your time.

So I cannot agree with you that nothing is new. However, because we live in an ever-changing universe, I must agree that nothing is permanent. No two consecutive days are exactly the same. Whereas you obviously felt weighed down by the monotony of a world in which everything seemed to be going round in cycles, with the same old things returning again and again, we today sometimes wish we could have a short break from change to enable us to catch our breath. Though it may seem paradoxical to say so, we find that about the only permanent thing is the process of change itself.

I see that I shall have to revise my thoughts about the appearance of new things. If it has been an error, why do you think I made it?

It's now becoming clear to me that you experienced the passage of time rather differently from the way we do. Your view of time is what we now call "cyclic," and it was widespread if not universal in ancient times. Of course our own experience of time is cyclic in part, for we readily recognize and empathize with your observations of the annual round of the seasons and of human generations following one another in quick succession.

But unlike you, Ecclesiastes, we couple cyclic time with a very strong awareness of linear time, for we look backward to a beginning that will never be repeated and forward to some kind of an end in the far distant future. This means that each moment in time is unique, for we never pass through the same moment twice. But as I've just said, we also experience weekly, monthly and annual cycles, and therefore it is perhaps more correct to describe our experience of time as a spiral. Mondays succeed one another every seven days, but no two Mondays, and no two New Year's Days are identical. It is because we experience time as a spiral, and not simply a series of cycles, that new things are forever appearing.

In the light of this I now invite you to tell me the way you see time.

You may recall that I expressed my understanding of time in the form of a little poem. Here it is:

Everything has its predestined moment,
every affair on earth its appropriate time.
There's a time to be born and a time to die,
a time to plant and a time to uproot,
a time to kill and a time to heal,
a time to knock down and a time to build up,
a time to cry and a time to laugh,
a time to wail and a time to dance about,

> *a time to fling stones away and a time to gather them together,*
> *a time to embrace and a time to refrain from embracing,*
> *a time to search and a time to leave lost,*
> *a time to keep and a time to throw away,*
> *a time to tear up and a time to stitch together,*
> *a time to be silent and a time to speak,*
> *a time to love and a time to hate,*
> *a time for war and a time for peace.*

Ecclesiastes, you may be interested to know that the poem you've just recited has become your most widely known observation, and the words are often quoted. But they don't quite answer the question about time that I asked you. Admittedly, time is not an easy phenomenon to understand, even though we live in it and all life depends on it. One of our great Western thinkers, St. Augustine, once remarked that he knew exactly what time was until he began to reflect on it.

What you've described to me, in this polarized way, is the succession of activities in which we humans may engage during the continuous flow of time. You have, no doubt correctly, asserted that each of these activities has its legitimate place. But when you speak of "a time," do you mean that each of these activities is already fixed beforehand and is quietly awaiting its appointed time to occur?

*As I said, **everything has its predestined moment.***

That statement suggests that you think everything is fixed beforehand. Such a view of life, commonly called determinism, has had a long history in Western thought. The strict determinist believes that what we take to be free will is an illusion and that in actual fact we do not exercise any freedom of choice at all. There are several varieties of determinism—theological, physical, philosophical and psychological. Your own Hebrew prophet Jeremiah showed himself something of a theological determinist when he asserted that even before he was born, God had preordained him to be a prophet—and that try as he might, he could not get out of it. The Protestant reformer John

Calvin, who thought our ultimate destiny is already fixed in the mind of God, called this concept *predestination.*

However, I'm not convinced you were such a complete determinist as that. So let me know what conclusion you arrived at yourself after reciting the many activities it is possible for a person to engage in?

Very well; looking at it that way, I am probably not a determinist, though the term is not familiar to me. I am more concerned with what all the activity adds up to in the end; the important issue is what happens as a result of all that a person does. As I said, **what does the doer himself stand to gain from all the hard work he has invested?**

If you are asking me, my initial answer is that we gain personal satisfaction from work that has produced useful results. But if you don't regard your accomplishments to be a source of personal gratification, what have you found out about people's efforts and goals in your study of human activities?

What have I found? They are all as futile as chasing after the wind, like a crookedness that cannot be made straight, or a void that cannot be filled.

You keep on using this word *hevel,* which in this context is best translated as "futile." But why do you think all human activities are so futile?

I have found that all we do has no permanent result. Think of it this way: **What do we humans have to show for our life's work, for all efforts in this world, for all our sweat and toil? One generation passes away and another takes its place.**

It's true enough that "one generation passes away and another takes its place," but does that really mean that all human achievements are worthless? To be sure, however much joy or satisfaction we experience when we bring an activity to a successful conclusion, that feeling slowly lessens as the accomplishment recedes into the past. Perhaps what you are deploring is the lack of permanence in our sense of achievement. The books we write become dated. The architectural wonders we erect eventually fall into decay. Most of us are forgotten two or three generations after we die. And even though a few famous people's names are preserved on monuments or in an encyclopaedia, the time will come when those, too, will become obsolete and be replaced.

So I suppose I must rather reluctantly agree with you that there is nothing permanent about any of our achievements. All of us will eventually be forgotten. Certainly it does make us wonder whether, in the long run, our individual lives make any real difference after all. What do you think about that?

*What I think is this—**It's only the earth that goes on forever.***

It's curious you should say that, for we've come rather recently to recognize that not even the earth will go on forever. Our astronomers tell us that in some four billion years this planet will be absorbed into the ever expanding but dying sun and that, long before that time, our human species will most likely have disappeared forever. Of course, as I said earlier, we know the earth is only a tiny fragment of the vast universe, whereas for you they were virtually one and the same. Even so, this new truth about the earth is but a further example of your affirmation of the impermanence of everything.

Because, as you so rightly say, nothing that we do lasts forever, it is all the more surprising—as you earlier observed—that we still have your words after more than two millennia. It is probable, however, that, if they had not been included in the Bible, they would have vanished long ago, just as all other trace of you has already disappeared.

At the beginning I asked you to tell more about yourself but all I've been able to learn is this. You were a Jewish sage who assumed the persona of King Solomon and took the title of the Proclaimer. I am very glad we still have your words, for they have not only survived to this point in earthly time but they often seem to me to be uncannily modern.

And what I've learned from you is that I am a biblical heretic, an early empiricist and a freethinker—terms I had never heard of before.

Yet, you leave me with this problem. You said "It's only the earth that goes on forever." In view of the fact that you spoke quite frequently about God, I would have expected you to say "It's only God who goes on forever." When next we talk I should like to discuss what you mean by "God" and how you understand God's relationship with us and with the earth.

4

WHAT DO YOU
MEAN BY 'GOD'?

Ecclesiastes, I want to find out how you understand God. On the one hand you are the only Jewish sage who never once referred to Yahweh. As you know, that's the personal name of the god peculiar to the Jewish people, a word we have usually translated into English as "the LORD." On the other hand you refer to God thirty-six times. Clearly God, if not Yahweh, is very important to you.

What I want to know is this. When you speak of God, are you referring to a supposed supernatural being who thinks, plans and retains ultimate control of the world? To put it bluntly, how would you respond to an evangelical Christian who asked you "Do you believe in a personal God?"

I have never heard God referred to as "personal," for such a term would bring God down to our personal or human level. How I understand God is very simple. Gods are gods and humans are humans. **God is in the sky and you are on the earth.**

We have long been familiar with the idea of God being in the sky for it is clearly expressed in the well known words of what Christians call the Lord's Prayer—"Our Father who art in heaven" and in your language the same word means both "sky" and "heaven." So my evangelical friends will be delighted to hear your response and will claim that you are a genuine theist after all.

What do you mean by theist?

Theists conceive God to be a supreme being who feels, thinks and acts much as we humans do, but on the grand scale. They believe he created the world and continues to control it from his dwelling-place in heaven above. You seemed to imply that when you said "God is in the sky." It was easy for you to speak of God as being in the sky above, since (as I said earlier) you are a "flat-earther."

But ever since Galileo led us into the modern space age some four hundred years ago, the dwelling-place for God in the sky has vanished; it has been swallowed up in what we understand as the vast expanding universe. Moreover, there is no longer any "outside" to the universe. The idea of God as a spiritual being in the sky does not make any sense to us today.

*So for you it is not true to say that **God is in the sky?***

Certainly not! And that brings me to a further reason I'm keen to explore how you understand God. The very concept of God has become problematical in our world today. Many people reject the notion of God altogether (to say nothing of a plurality of gods) and declare themselves atheists. You are clearly not an atheist or you wouldn't speak of God at all.

But it's the way you speak of God that puzzles me. You use the word *elohim*. Now, that's a plural noun. Biblical authors sometimes used to refer to the gods of the nations, and then it *is* plural. But it is also used in the Bible to refer to Yahweh, the god of Israel, and then it is regarded as singular. But it's not a proper name like Yahweh, even though we've long treated it as such. In most cases you seem to use the word in its singular sense, but sometimes you put "the" in front of it, as if to mean "the gods." So when you use the term *elohim*, are you referring to "the gods" in a rather general way or are you speaking of one particular god?

I was simply reflecting what I hear people saying. Some say "the gods" and some say "God." I had no special reason for distinguishing one usage of the word from the other.

Well then, do you think of God in the same way as your fellow Jews do in their Scriptures? There they declare that their God, Yahweh, chose the Jewish people to be his special people, delivered them from slavery under the Pharaohs, and then established the Davidic dynasty to rule them. As a Jew you must be familiar with your cultural inheritance, but though you speak of God often, you make no mention of those historical events that Jews celebrate as "acts of God." I would like you to tell me how you understood God to be related to us and to the world?

*As I said before, **God is in the sky and you are on the earth.
That means that God transcends us, since he is above us.
And as for what he does in the world, Consider the works of
God, and ask yourself whether anyone can straighten what he
has made crooked?***

So you simply refuse to speak of the "mighty acts of God" that your fellow Jews make so much of. They believe God makes himself known by what he does in history. But when I ask you about this, you immediately change the subject from historical events to the way the physical world operates. How come?

*My chief concern was not to speculate on possible unseen
worlds that I could not observe, but to set down my reflections
on our human life in the here and now.*

Yet you evidently assume that God is the one responsible for the way the world is made. I gather from this that you understand God primarily as the Creator. That way of explaining your understanding of God is rather like what our philosophers call the cosmological argument. It goes like this: "Because the world exists, it must be the work of someone, and that someone we call God." At the popular level this argument still carries a good deal of weight in our culture.

And I can see why, for it seems quite self-evident to me.

Your statement also implies that there is an unbridgeable gulf between the power of God and the puny efforts of us humans.

As you say, we cannot straighten what he has made crooked. In other words, we humans cannot possibly change what God has made. But here's the problem—why did he make some things crooked? Worse yet, why does he bring about things that harm us—things like storms, earthquakes, droughts and famines?

That's like asking "Why are things are as they are?" I do not consider that to be a question we humans can ever answer. We must surely just accept reality as it is. What we can *do is to try to understand it and work out the most appropriate way to respond to it.* **In the days when you prosper rejoice; and in the days you suffer adversity . . .**

Ecclesiastes, excuse me for interrupting, but I want to know where God fits into our prosperity and adversity.

As I was about to say, **consider this: God is as responsible for the one as for the other, and manages things in such a way that we humans have no clue as to how he works.**

As you see it, then, we must simply accept what happens to us in the world, no matter what it is, because that's the way God works. When his works treat us well—with sunshine, bumper harvests and good health—we must rejoice; and when our harvests fail because of drought or there is a downturn in the economy (to use our modern equivalent), we must simply take it on the chin, for that's the way God works in the world.

That notion reminds me of a passage in the Book of Isaiah, in which some unknown prophet put these words into the mouth of God: "I form light and I create darkness. I bring prosperity and I create disasters." I'm sure you'd agree with that and also with the saying that "God makes his sun rise on the evil and on the good, and sends his rain on the just and on the unjust."

I do indeed, but who made that last observation?

Those are the words of Jesus of Nazareth. He was a Jewish sage who taught in Galilee some centuries after you. You and he had more in common than is usually realised. I shall probably refer to him again, for a great new religion called Christianity sprang up around him and his teaching. But at the moment let's not be sidetracked from the issue I wish to pursue with you.

The idea that God bears responsibility for evil as well as good raises serious moral problems. If his works in the world both sustain and destroy us, does this God you speak of really care about us humans? Can he even be said to be good? My theistic friends maintain that God *is* good and wills for us only what is best for us; they put their faith in what they call "divine providence" and insist that God would never deliberately harm us.

How then do they explain the evils that befall us?

They regard misfortune as a form of divine punishment sent for our ultimate good. When a natural disaster occurs, such as a recent tsunami that drowned hundreds of thousands of holiday-makers, they ask themselves what they have done wrong. Even our insurance companies used to describe such calamities as "acts of God" and refused to pay compensation. On the other hand, if a supposed "act of God" is to our advantage, as when a mortally ill person is restored to health, theists call it a miracle.

I know nothing of what you call "divine providence" and I'm even puzzled by your term "miracle." Can you explain it more clearly to me?

The term "miracle" used to mean a marvellous and unusual event that could not be readily ascribed to any human or natural cause. In modern times, because we now know a great deal about what we call the laws of nature, it has taken on a new meaning: "the temporary suspension of the laws of nature." This idea has led to much religious debate. Theists claim that, since God ordained the laws of nature, he can suspend them whenever he wishes, while non-theists deny that any such miracles ever take place.

I've never heard of any "laws of nature" but I do know what it means to marvel. I believe we should marvel at everything God *does, both good and bad. As I've often said, we should **simply stand in awe of God. For he is responsible for both the prosperity and the adversity we suffer.***

So you are not an atheist, but neither are you a theist, for you don't believe in miracles in the way they do. You do not interpret all natural events as the acts of a loving God that must be interpreted as either blessings or punishments. Since you believe God created the world and is hence responsible for both the prosperity and the adversity that we suffer just because of the way he made it, perhaps we should call you a deist.

A what? Still another new term for me? What do you mean by deist?

That term means one who believes it was God who created the universe at the beginning of time, but thereafter never interfered with it again. There are no miracles or "acts of God." The God of the deists is one who simply lets the world run its course according to the physical laws he provided for it at its beginning.

*Since that term is new to me I cannot tell whether I'm a deist or not. Certainly I understand God to have created the world but as I see it, **God manages things in such a way that we humans have no clue as to how he works** or why.*

Now you really have me puzzled. On the one hand you refer to all things that happen in the natural world, whether good or harmful to us, as the "works of God." On the other hand you confess that it is impossible for us to discover any clue as to *how* God works. Surely this casts real doubt on whether God has ever been at work at all! I must ask you, therefore, why you regard everything that happens in the natural world as the works of God, if you are ready to concede that nothing in the world can actually confirm this.

Please remember that in our last discussion we established that you are an empiricist, one who bases his convictions on what he sees or experiences. So let me ask you this: why do you refer to everything that happens in the world, for better or for worse, as "the works of God"? Indeed, why do you speak of God at all?

*It is because **I've observed the activities that God has provided to keep humankind fully occupied.***

But here, Ecclesiastes, you've once again sidestepped my question; in fact you remind me of some of our more evasive politicians! You ignored my query as to why you speak of God at all. Apparently you simply assume the reality of God without thinking about it any further. Though in your book you seem to be challenging many popular notions, you never question the reality of God. I suspect that you probably agree with your psalmist who said, "It's only the fool who says, 'There is no God.'"

Certainly I do. The reality of God seems to me to be as self-evident as the reality of the world itself.

So God has become for you the simplest way of explaining why there is a world at all and why all things are as they are. And when you study the many different activities that humans occupy themselves with, you affirm without any further explanation that is just the way God has planned life for us human beings.

*Just so! **He made everything just right for its own proper time.***

Your words remind me of what we read in the Book of Genesis: "God looked at what he had made and behold it was very good!" But is everything just right? Can we really say that the world is very good? Certainly we depend on the fruits of the earth that he supposedly made, but in your view he is also responsible for the earthquakes, droughts, famines and other disasters from which we suffer. Does that mean that you judge earthquakes and droughts to be good? Surely this needs clarifying; you'll need to tell me more.

Clearly, God causes the earthquakes and the droughts. But not to harm us or punish us, indeed not for any particular purpose at all. That's just the way God works.

So the works of God serve no particular purpose so far as we humans are concerned.

No, not unless you find some purpose in this further observation that I made: **God put the everlasting universe itself into the human mind, but in such a way that people cannot discover from beginning to end what it is that God has done.**

I find that to be a very profound statement and I need time to digest it slowly. You've just used a word that both puzzles and excites me—*'olam.* We don't have a word that quite matches it. In the time when you were writing, it had come to mean the age or the world in which we live. (Indeed, in the modern Hebrew spoken in Israel, it simply means "the world.") But in earlier times the word 'olam also contained the idea of eternity, and that's why you used it in our last discussion when you said "It's only the earth that goes on *forever*." So I've translated it here as "everlasting universe."

That makes your observation one of quite remarkable insight. It recognizes how the human mind can not only understand the concept of eternity, but also construct a mental picture of the whole universe ("everything that is"). That was an extraordinary thought to have had in your day. It captures a fact to which too few people even today devote sufficient thought. And yet you reached that conclusion all those centuries ago.

I feel both gratified and humbled that you think so.

In our day your observation has become even more awe-inspiring, for the modern explosion of knowledge challenges us to attempt to hold in our minds a vastly enlarged mental picture of the universe. Today our knowledge of how the universe began and of how life evolved on this planet from small beginnings has caused us to be even more aware that we are the products of what we often call Nature.

Nature? I have never heard of such a term. Can you explain it?

By "Nature" we mean the original or ongoing state of things. We mean the heavenly bodies in the sky and the way life manifests itself on the earth. We mean the plants, flowers and trees. We mean the fish in the sea, the birds in the air, the insects and the animals on the earth. The reason you've not heard of "Nature" is because in the Hebrew language of your day there was no word equivalent to it.

Perhaps that's because you still lived in the shadow of the ancient times when people believed that everything to be observed by us—including such events as storms, earthquakes, droughts, spring growth and so on—were originated and controlled by unseen gods and spirits. Indeed that's how your word *elohim* came about; it originally referred to the spiritual forces assumed to be responsible for everything the ancients observed happening in the world that neither humans nor animals had caused. Today we call them the works of nature. But you called them the works of *elohim*.

But who then invented the term "elohim"? And if the elohim could not be seen, how did people come to know about them?

The answer to that lies in the complex and still largely unknown story of how all human language slowly evolved, and that took a very long time. All this is of course wholly new to you, for as the story of Adam and Eve illustrates, people of your day assumed not only that all things were created merely a few thousand years earlier, but also that language itself was created by God along with the people who spoke it.

We think very differently now. And as for the term *elohim*, we suspect that when your ancient ancestors created the idea, they were, without knowing it, projecting their own human thoughts onto the forces of nature. They assumed that everything that they saw occurring must be alive or else moved by an unseen force. Further, since they experienced some natural events as being erratic and unpredictable, they naturally conceived of the gods as being capricious, often irrational in their decisions, sometimes immoral in their behaviour, and occasionally even vengeful towards mere humans. That's why they perceived the works of *elohim* as alternately beneficial and harmful, just as you've said.

All that about the origin of the term "elohim" is strange to me, of course, and not at all easy for me to absorb. But if "elohim" once referred to many gods, how is it that I have come often to understand the word to refer to a single being?

Well, that's mainly due to your Jewish prophets. They eventually laughed those multiple gods out of court. They even used your own favourite word, *hevel,* which means "having no substance," to declare that "the gods" had no reality at all. Having rejected them, the prophets proclaimed that all of the non-human forces that transcend us comprise a unity. This transition from the "many" to the "one" was still proceeding in your day; and that's why, as I observed earlier, you sometimes seemed to be referring to the gods and sometimes to God.

But why did we Jewish people still continue to use the term "elohim" after the many gods had, as you say, been so thoroughly rejected by the prophets and replaced by the One?

You may well ask! Today it seems odd that you Jews continued to use the same word *elohim* to refer this divine unity. But that's just one example of the many unexplainable things that occur in the evolution of language. In any case, you Jews still possessed the term Yahweh to help you in the transition—though as I noted earlier you yourself avoided its use. To this day your Jewish successors express this radical transition in what they call the Shema, part of which declares " Yahweh, our *elohim*, is *one*." And as soon as it came to be believed that there is only one deity, it became the practice to treat the word "god" as a proper name; and therefore we usually write its first letter as a capital.

But I never regarded elohim as a proper name, in the same way as Yahweh is.

That's what I'm just now beginning to find out. You use the word almost in its original sense—the gods—except that you always treat it as a singular word. It seems to me that your references to *elohim* indicate a way of thinking that you fall back on when you want to say something very basic about the world at large. Since *elohim* literally means "the gods," it's a term that would have been understood in all the cultures known to you. Indeed, perhaps as a result of our general knowledge of the Greek and Roman gods, we sometimes hear people say in casual conversation such things as, "Ye gods!" or "The gods are not smiling on us today." Also, we sometimes speak of the world as "Creation," in much the same way as you speak of "everything that is" as the work of *elohim*.

In this respect you remind me of some of our great scientific thinkers such as Einstein. Although Jewish, he was no theist; and yet he said, "I want to know God's thoughts. The rest are details." Likewise the physicist Paul Davies is by no means a theist, and yet he entitled his book on science and the search for meaning as *The Mind of God*. When any of our modern scientists resort to God-talk, they are using this ancient word symbolically. Since they often say they are looking for what they call a "Theory of Everything" they naturally fall back on the word "God," since it long served the same purpose. In a similar way, it seems to me, you also treat the word "God" as a symbol to refer to the way things are in the world. To put it yet more simply, "the ways of God" that you earlier asked me to consider are simply what we today call "the laws of nature."

I need some time to get used to this strange new term "nature." So you'll need to explain to me what you mean by "the laws of nature."

I can do this best by reminding you of your own observations of the various cycles of natural events that we talked about in our last dialogue. They illustrate your clear discernment of order in the world. And despite its numerous random or even chaotic characteristics, modern scientists have been learning much more about the physical world's underlying consistency—a pattern of regularity they refer to as "the laws of nature." You are to be congratulated on that insight, for it was breaking new ground. I suggest that it came to you because your own Jewish culture had led you to regard *elohim* as a unity.

Thank you for your kind words, but you give me credit for something I'm not aware of. Why do you see my observations as something new?

Well, during the long period when the ancients believed the world to be controlled by a plurality of unpredictable gods they remained blind to its underlying order. It was only after the *elohim* came to be conceived as one, that they began to look for some unity or consistency in the "works of God." The many gods that people had earlier believed in could readily be conceived as acting at cross-purposes with one another, and thus creating the apparent disorder in the world. But as soon as all earthly phenomena were to be attributed to only one divine source, it was difficult to imagine this one all-powerful God to be in conflict with himself. So people began to look for some order behind the apparent disorder. Do you remember how the first Book of Moses begins?

Of course I do. "In the beginning of God's creation of the heaven and the earth, all was shapeless and chaotic."

If we interpret that verse symbolically, it describes very clearly what I'm getting at. Everything under the gods was disorderly and chaotic. But now that the one Creator God has brought order out of chaos, we can rely on an underlying unity or rational order in the world itself despite its often unruly appearance. Among other things, then, "God" can be thought of as the name for that cosmic order.

Indeed, some of today's scientists claim that modern empirical science owes its very foundation to the emergence of monotheism—the belief that the world owed its existence to the one creative force that we call God. This led in due course to the idea of cosmic order and it is that which our scientists have been uncovering and enunciating as the laws of nature, the term that you now ask me about.

All this new information simply amazes me. But can you tell me whether any Jews are among those scientists?

Of course! I've already mentioned Albert Einstein. But I must also tell you about the philosopher Baruch Spinoza. You'll recognize by his first name that he was a Jew. He lived in seventeenth-century Holland, just as empirical science was beginning to develop. Because of his understanding of God he became known as the father of pantheism. This term literally means that God is viewed as the sum-total of everything. Whereas theists say "God *made* everything," pantheists say "God *is* everything." Spinoza's most famous phrase was "God or Nature," by which he implied that he regarded the two words as more or less synonymous.

Now let me make a suggestion to you. Since I find your understanding of *elohim* very close to Spinoza's, I'd like to take the liberty of translating your use of the word *elohim* as "Nature" whenever that seems appropriate. I think it would be instructive to go back and hear some of your observations using this new translation.

Consider the works of Nature, and ask yourself whether anyone can straighten what it has made crooked.

And now that remarkable insight of yours.

And then Nature put the everlasting universe itself into the human mind, but in such a way that people cannot discover from beginning to end how Nature did it.

Yes! You see, that supports my tentative conclusion that you might have used the word "Nature" if you had possessed such a word. Perhaps you will offer some further examples of what you said.

*Nature has so arranged matters that people may stand in awe
of it. Whatever exists has already been, and what is yet to exist
has already been; for Nature always seeks to repeat the past.*

Excellent! It's clear that when you use the term *elohim* you're
nearly always talking about the way things are in the natural
world. This is why you drew attention to the way natural events
occur in cycles. Here you do it again when you say "Nature always seeks to repeat the past." We ourselves often say of some
phenomenon that we observe, "That's Nature's way." So what
you attribute to *elohim* is what we commonly attribute to Nature.
Can you give me one more example of how you understand
your word for God, now translated as Nature?

*I believe that whatever Nature produces will surely endure
forever. For to it nothing can be added and from it nothing
can be taken away.*

That's an impressive statement. It could have been made in
our century, for it's just what our scientists say about the sum-
total of energy in the universe, and energy is the basic stuff of
which all material objects are composed. Thus in many of the
contexts where you refer to "God," the word "Nature" seems to
me its precise equivalent.

*It may sound right to you, but because the word "Nature" is
so foreign to me it makes little sense to me to speak of God as
Nature. I wonder if you are putting words into my mouth and
making me say things I never intended.*

Even though I stand by my translation, I partly accept your rebuke, for you remind me that even if you had possessed a word
for Nature, it could not have meant for you quite what it means
to us. The fact that we live in very different worlds makes translation of language very difficult, if not sometimes impossible.
Before I go further in translating your references to "God" as
"Nature," then, let me explain to you more fully when we next
talk just how we today see the world of nature.

5

NATURE AND US

Ecclesiastes, I'm glad to have this opportunity to explain to you how we understand Nature today. As I pointed out when we first talked, your view of the world we humans live in was very different from ours. You told me you saw the sky above as the place where God dwells. But we regard the sky as an immeasurable space in which we see planets, stars and distant galaxies. The earth itself is one of several planets revolving around the sun and the sun is simply one of the billions of stars you see in the sky.

Further, the space-time continuum—as we now call the universe—is not at all static in the way you conceived the world to be. We have discovered that it is continuously changing. Not only is it expanding in size, but, on this planet at least, an incredible variety of life has been evolving over billions of years. In one sense, therefore, we can say that the universe keeps changing as if it were alive.

Hold on a minute! You're going too fast. This is all so bewildering that my head is whirling. The world as I know it does not change. As I said earlier, even though its events occur in cycles, nothing is ever really new. Please tell me what you mean by "evolving."

Well, the idea of evolution is new, even for us. And since there is no hint of it in the Bible, those who turn to the Bible for the final truth still strongly reject the notion. Perhaps the best way I can explain evolution to you is first to draw your attention to the way a small seed can grow and develop into a large tree, for that's something you can see and observe for yourself; and, as you've told me, you prefer to base your beliefs on what you can see.

Then observe that the seed does not grow because of any creative force outside of it. Provided it can draw upon water and nourishment from its surroundings, the seed clearly has within itself the capacity to develop into a tree. Now use your imagination and transfer that image of developing growth to all life on this planet. The modern sciences have given us good reason to believe that all kinds of planetary life, whether plants or animate creatures, have developed out of earlier and simpler forms, going right back to a point where something alive emerged out of very complex non-living matter. This is what we call the process of evolution. All life developed, or evolved as we say, in relation to its environment. This is the new knowledge that we call ecology.

That explanation strikes me as too fantastic to be possible. No wonder many of your people refuse to believe it and regard all life forms as fixed, just as I do.

I agree that the evolution of life on this planet seems at first almost impossible to believe, but is it any less extraordinary than the ability of a small seed to turn into a big tree? Even more breath-taking is the growth of a fertilized ovum into an intelligent human being! Indeed, the growth of each one of us from conception to adult maturity may be said to recapitulate in a single lifetime the evolution of the human species over a very long time, from the simplest of living creatures to what we are today.

But the growth of a tree is something that I can observe for myself during my lifetime.

Just so, and because you've seen it take place many times, you take it for granted without realising what a wonderful process it is. The process of evolution we find harder to accept mainly because our imaginations have difficulty coping with the enormous period of time it required—some three billion years.

Yet the evolution of life on this planet must in turn be placed within the much larger process of cosmic evolution for that took even longer.

Cosmic evolution! What on earth are you talking about?

I'm referring to the expanding development of the whole universe or what we sometimes call the cosmos. Scientists now tell us that it came into existence about fifteen billion years ago with what they call the "Big Bang." That was the moment when time itself began with an enormous explosion of energy, the name we give to the basic substance of which all material objects are composed. The energy of the cosmos has the innate power to form itself into ever more complex designs, from atoms to molecules, from molecules to mega-molecules, from mega-molecules to cells, from cells to organisms, such as living creatures.

Since all I know about is what we call dust, I find those terms very strange.

And it must be just as strange for you to hear the stars in the sky being called nebulae, galaxies, super-novas and planets and to learn how staggeringly large they are and how many billions of them exist. Cosmic energy has been forming itself into these bodies ever since the "Big Bang." All of this, including the evolution of life on this planet, is what we now know as the natural world. The more we have come to know about how nature works, the less need there has been to postulate a divine creator. Nature is self-creative and its self-designing potential is truly awe-inspiring. Thus Nature itself achieves, through its own inherent power and patterns of development, what theists have long attributed to God.

So that's why the philosopher Spinoza, whom you told me about, spoke of "God or Nature"?

Exactly! And the more we have learned about life on this planet, through such sciences as biology and geology, the more did people's ideas about God undergo change. Indeed, it has now become possible to write "the history of God." By that we mean the history of what the word "God" has meant to people in different times and places. Humans once thought Nature was alive, moving and operating according to the whims of the "the gods" who inhabited or controlled all visible natural phenomena. As we noted in our last discussion, this was the cultural context in which your word *elohim* originated.

*I confess I don't know what to make of all that, for the idea of things developing and evolving is strange to me. I have always said that **there is nothing new on the face of the earth.** It seemed to me to be self-evident that everything on earth had remained the same from its beginning.*

That's because you had little awareness of history. In a single lifetime, we experience such a tiny fragment of cosmic time that, despite the cyclical patterns of events we mentioned earlier, we are left with the impression of a changeless world. Just as animals appear to live out their lives in a kind of timeless present, so did the human species through most of its time on this planet. It was not until your era, by which time the human species had been evolving for more than a million years, that humans were at last beginning to develop a sense of history. A Greek writer called Herodotus, who lived a century before you, has been called the "father of history." Yet, even before him, your own Jewish scholars were also developing a historical sense as they began to compile the Torah and the Chronicles of the Kings. Why did you not give them more attention?

*As I told you, **I studied all human activities, everything that happens to people on the face of the earth.** I concerned myself with what I could observe and did not see what had gone before as having any further relevance.*

You remind me of a famous remark by Henry Ford, the great industrialist, when he said, "History is bunk!" You see, it's only quite recently that we've learned to attach great importance to history. Indeed our historical awareness is only a little older than our awareness of evolution, and the two are closely connected. Our new awareness of history has been tremendously illuminating, throwing new light on all sorts of subjects. Each of us has a history. Each culture and civilisation has a history. The universe has a history. And now we can say that God has a history.

Moreover, your own Jewish prophets played an important role in shaping that awareness when they replaced "the gods" with one God (whom you Jews somewhat paradoxically continued to call *elohim*). That radical change from many gods to one had far-reaching consequences, for it meant that as Creator of all things, God had to be wholly distinct from the physical universe he had supposedly created. Whereas "the gods" had once been conceived of as the living forces of Nature—and therefore *within* it—God the Creator was now imagined to be *external* to Nature.

Is that why I was led to believe that **God is in the sky***?*

It is indeed! Our new understanding of Nature means that the creative power long attributed to a God so distant as to be outside of the universe must now be seen as part of Nature itself. Some speak of this power that permeates Nature as its "life-force," in much the same way as you ancients used to speak of "spirit." But whatever terms we use, imagining it as an objective thing that can be differentiated from Nature is a serious mistake. Indeed, Nature has come to be so widely understood as a self-designing reality that some twentieth-century thinkers called "process theologians" identify God with the process of evolution itself.

In this history of God, as you call it, where would you place my thoughts about God?

It is clear that under the influence of the Jewish prophets you were moving beyond "the gods" of nature, for you used the term *elohim* as if you were speaking of a unity. But though you reveal some hints of the personal God, as later developed by Jewish, Christian, and Muslim theists, your God was more closely involved with nature than with the events of human history. That's why, many centuries later, we can judge you to be closer to Spinoza and the process theologians than to the theists.

Your place in the long and complex history of God helps me to understand why, when earlier I expected you to state that God alone is eternal, you said that only the earth lasts forever. I now see more clearly that the earth (or the world as you experienced it) is basic to your understanding of human existence, and that you recognize its reality and patterns of operation to transcend us humans and everything we do.

Of course! Recall what I have repeatedly said: **Stand in awe of Nature and do what it requires of you, for this is the whole duty of humankind.**

You have indeed, and now I can better see how you understand the word *elohim*. And your assertion is particularly pertinent to us in the twenty-first century. At the very time when belief in the traditional "God in heaven" has ceased to be meaningful, we are rediscovering how the natural world still transcends us—and this in spite of our knowledge explosion and complex technology. We are being forced to relearn that it is Nature that we must hold in awe.

We entered the twentieth century imagining ourselves to be fast becoming the masters of nature. For centuries we had been encouraged in this enterprise by the biblical injunction, "Be fruitful and multiply and subdue the earth and have dominion over every living thing." I'm sure you recognize this text from the very first chapter of the Torah. Yet I notice you make no mention of it. Perhaps, like Spinoza, you saw God and the natural world so closely allied that any attempt by us humans to dominate nature would be blasphemous, an act of hubris tantamount to challenging the might of God. Did you not warn me about this when you invited me to consider the works of God?

You mean when I said, **Can anyone straighten what Nature has made crooked?**

Exactly. Since, in your understanding, the works of God are the works of Nature, we humans cannot change them. That brings me back to what I noted earlier: this must be why you never seem to connect this God with Moses, or with the prophets, or with any of the events of history.

The works of God (or Nature as you are teaching me to say) are visible for us all to see. They are entirely different from the events we humans are involved in, for it is we who are responsible for the latter, both the good and the bad. They are not the works of God.

Now this is most unusual for a Jew. The Torah, so highly respected by the Jews, shows that they understood God to have chosen them as his people and entered into a covenant with them. No Jew could be ignorant of that, since in the course of every year the Torah is read from beginning to end in weekly portions every Sabbath. It's strange that you've made no mention of this. That prompts me to ask you directly: What was your attitude toward the temple and the synagogue, the places where God was worshipped? Was it your practice to frequent either of them?

All I want to say in answer to that question is this: **Watch your step when you go to the house of God.**

You seem reluctant even to name either the temple or the synagogue. Instead you reply with a very general term—"the house of God." That could refer to any place people regard as holy. What is even more surprising is the warning tone of your response. Why is that?

What I have come to learn is this: **Being ready to understand is better than offering sacrifice.**

I gather from what you say, Ecclesiastes, that you seldom if ever went to the Jerusalem temple, for that was the one and only place where Jews customarily offered sacrifices. Indeed, you appear to have had a rather low opinion of what went on there. Of course, you were not the first of your people to be critical of the sacrifices, for they had been condemned by some of the prophets who went before you. And, after your times, the sage Jesus is said to have stirred up the ire of the priests by attempting to cleanse the temple of its blatant commercialism. About the same time a group of Jewish pietists we know of as the Essenes of the Qumran Community deemed what went on at the Temple so abhorrent that they withdrew from traditional Jewish practices altogether and created new rites of their own down at the Dead Sea.

I would go even further than these Essenes you speak of and say, **Being ready to understand is better than offering sacrifice with fools who haven't even the brains to do any real evil.**

So you are critical not only of religious rites; you speak scathingly of those who offer sacrifices, whether priests or lay people, and even declare them to be brainless. Your rather extreme statement reminds me of some of the Protestant Reformers of the Christian Church only five hundred years ago. They took strong exception to the sacrifice of the body of Christ being re-enacted on the altar in the Christian ceremony known as the mass. They even condemned it as mindless mumbo-jumbo (much as you do) because it was performed in the Latin language that the common people could not understand.

In like manner you say it is more important to act with some understanding of what you are doing. Of course that's why the Reformers replaced the mass with a ceremony in the language of the people. And the dominant element of that tended to be a lengthy sermon that explained the essential Christian message. I imagine that's a change you would have approved of?

Not wholly! What I say is this. **Be in no hurry to speak, and do not think of uttering anything hastily before God.**

What? You are even cautious of speech in "the house of God"? But rabbis have been doing that in synagogues from your day to the present. Even your fellow sage Jesus occasionally spoke in the synagogue. Another fellow Jew, known to us as St. Paul, did not hesitate to preach his message in the synagogues. Indeed priests and ministers have been doing that regularly in churches ever since.

But please note that I said, **do not think of uttering anything hastily** *before God.*

Aha, I see I misconstrued your words. Your intention was to warn us against hasty and careless speech in the act of worship. Perhaps you intended your warning to apply particularly to the preacher who believes or pretends that he is proclaiming the absolute and final truth on God's behalf. If so, I imagine you'd take a very dim view of much that has gone on in pulpits in the last few centuries, for Protestant preachers often capitalized on the sermon's central place in the service to give the impression they knew the will of their God even better than God knew it himself. But if you do not advocate speech as an adequate replacement for the sacrifices that you condemn, what would you commend?

If you ask me for my advice, I reply with something very simple. **The best that any of us can do is to eat and drink and enjoy ourselves in our work.**

It's quite a shock to hear you say that. It is very like some words we associate with the Greek philosopher Epicurus, "Eat, drink and be merry, for tomorrow we die." Strangely enough, he was probably your contemporary, for he established his school in Athens about the very time you were writing. It's a pity you two never met, for you'd have had much in common, as these very words show.

But at the moment I'm more interested in your claim that we humans have it within us to live and find satisfaction in what we do, without offering sacrifices at the temple or "going to church" to hear sermons. I don't think that either Bible-lovers or churchgoers will like to hear you say that. Humanists, of course, will rejoice in your words. Indeed, you sound like a humanist.

Now I find you calling me a humanist, in addition to the other titles you gave me, and I don't even know what humanism is.

The term goes back some centuries to what we call the Renaissance. Its leading thinkers became known as humanists, because when they studied the ancient Greek and Latin writers they re-discovered the creative potential in the human condition. This had long been denied by Christianity, which emphasized *ad nauseam* the sinful condition of the human species.

Today humanism can mean different things to different people. So let me give you a philosophical definition—humanism is any philosophy of life that recognizes the dignity of the human condition, makes humankind itself the measure of all things and takes human nature, with its limits and interests, as its theme. This is what you seem to be doing in your observations about life.

*I suppose you think that because I said **I studied all human activities, everything that happens to people on the face of the earth.***

That's true, but I also notice you made no reference to the religious activities that humans engage in, except to speak scathingly about offering sacrifices. Do you not think that we all stand in need of some form of spiritual practice or discipline if we are going to succeed in living the good life? Christians have long believed that inherent sinfulness prevented them from living according to God's will and thus leading a happy and satisfying life. Their leaders taught them that they first needed to be reconciled to God, and it was to accomplish this end that they went to church. As one who seems to have avoided the temple and the synagogue, how do you propose we can live a satisfying life without receiving some external help?

We humans have our own inner resources to turn to. If they fail, we can turn to one another for help. **Indeed, it's possible for all people to eat and drink, and find satisfaction in everything they do.**

I'm agreeably surprised to hear you say that, particularly in view of so much else you have written in your book. But does happiness come that easily?

I don't say that it comes easily, but I do say that it is possible. And the reason for that? **It is a gift from Nature.**

So you believe that happiness should come to us quite naturally, as if it were a gift we receive simply by virtue of having been born. That would certainly put an end to the whole idea of original sin that shaped Christianity for so long. Christian theologians appealed to the Jewish Scriptures to prove that, even when we are born, we are sinful. They quoted the words of your Psalmist, "In sin did my mother conceive me." You obviously disagree with him and regard the newborn child as unblemished, since you believe we humans are born with the potential to live a happy life.

This too, I realised, is from the hand of Nature. For if it were not for it, who could eat or who could have any enjoyment?

I notice that you sometimes refer to Nature in personal terms. Most of the time it is unclear whether you think of God (or Nature, as I think you mean) in personal or impersonal terms, for in the Hebrew language every noun is either feminine or non-feminine. Anything non-feminine, such as your references to God, could be what we who speak English would understand as either "it" or "he." But here at last you speak of the "hand" of Nature and the "gifts" of Nature. But I suspect this is no more than metaphoric language, just as we may choose to speak of the gifts of Mother Nature. You see, it is our custom also to speak of Nature as our Mother, but for you Nature is either male or neuter.

I can see that these differences in language do more than cause confusion; they shape the very way we perceive reality!

Yes, indeed, and here they demand that we clarify the issue at hand. As you rightly point out, we know how to eat and drink from the time we are born because Nature has shaped us that way. But Nature cannot always be regarded as motherly, or else there would be no natural disasters. So does Nature distribute his or its gifts quite indiscriminately? How come some people enjoy life to the full while others live in almost constant misery, and apparently through no fault of their own?

Ah, what an evil burden Nature has given to the human race to busy itself with!

You agree, then, that Nature is quite amoral and shows no special interest in or care for us humans. In that case, unlike theists, we cannot expect any special help from Nature in times of adversity as they do from their personal God. As you've said, we must simply accept the bad with the good, for that's just the way Nature works. What was it that finally convinced you of this rather disturbing fact?

*Quite a number of things really. But in particular, **I looked again and saw all the oppression that was taking place on the earth. Moreover, I detected a reason for this: human hearts are full of evil.***

So you now concede that though Nature brings us into the world as innocent and sinless creatures, we can develop evil hearts through our own wilful choices. In other words, though Nature endows us with gifts, it's up to us how we use them, and when we get ourselves into difficulties Nature will not intervene to save us. Although you speak of the hand and the gifts of Nature, this does not imply that Nature has any personal love for us humans.

No, certainly not. Nature does not play favourites!

Therefore learning how to live the good and satisfying life is by no means easy and straightforward. Since you have observed a great deal of suffering and unfairness during your lifetime, I suggest that in our next meeting we turn our attention to the problems raised by the existence of evil and injustice in the world.

6

IS LIFE
UNFAIR?

Ecclesiastes, I'd like to talk with you about your deep concern over the injustice you find in the world. It became clear in our last discussions that when you speak of God you are referring chiefly to the way we see Nature operating in the world. When you speak of the "hand and the gifts of God," do you mean that Nature shows some sort of moral concern for us humans? Does Nature take any notice, for example, of whether a person does right or wrong?

Yes it does! **To the person who does well before it, Nature gives wisdom, knowledge and happiness.**

So though, as you indicated last time, you believe it is quite natural for people to achieve happiness by their own efforts, you think their eventual success in doing so is dependent on their living a good life. As you see it, that's just the way Nature works. It does not require Nature to intervene, as a personal God is thought by theists to do; rather it is quite *natural* for people to become wise and find happiness provided they always do what is good and right. But what about the people who don't do well?

Well they, *of course, do not fare well at all. As I said,* **to the sinner Nature gives the task of gathering and amassing wealth only to hand it over to the one who finds favour with it.**

In other words, when people suffer some unexpected disaster, it can be traced back to their own wrongdoing. Now that sounds only a little different from the conventional wisdom of theism.

As theists see it, God is always in control, rewarding or punishing people according to their deserts, but for you this sort of even-handed justice is just the way Nature works. But whereas *they* believe they can pray to God and ask for mercy, *you* understand Nature to be an impersonal power that makes no changes in response to prayer. Yet if Nature is so impersonal, how does it know the difference between good and bad behaviour?

I have often pondered that very question. You no doubt recall that I said, "Since there's a time for every affair and every activity, Nature will bring judgment to both the virtuous and the criminal."

But if you think the final outcomes of our actions are determined by the workings of an impersonal Nature, rather than by the moral decisions of a personal God, does that mean you see this world to be essentially a moral one where we can confidently expect some form of justice to be meted out? In other words, is it the way of Nature to respond to whether people do good or evil by ensuring that people always get their just deserts?

*Alas, I do not find this to be the case at all. At first I fully expected this to be a moral world where all receive their just deserts. But my hope was not fulfilled, and eventually I concluded this hope to be a vain one. **This also is meaningless—a mere chasing after the wind.***

So in spite of asserting earlier that Nature gives wisdom to those who do well and causes sinners to experience unexpected disasters, you've now changed your mind. What led you to do this?

*Here is the reason I concluded that this is not a moral world: **Wherever judgment for evil deeds is not carried out promptly, people's minds are filled with ideas of crime, and a malefactor may commit a hundred crimes and live a long life.***

So when you say that Nature brings judgment to both the virtuous and the criminal you are really referring to the fact that in our society it is natural for us humans to foster good behaviour and discourage bad behaviour by punishing evil deeds whenever we encounter them. In other words, Nature performs its works of judgment through us. Admittedly, as you've made clear elsewhere, we humans are all part of the natural world.

You seem now to be complaining that, though in accordance with Nature we should be its instruments of executing justice in the world, we don't always perform this function consistently. Thus the apparent morality meted out by Nature cannot be relied upon, for it does not operate consistently or absolutely. Theists, of course, believe that invariable and appropriate recompense for our behaviour is one of the hallmarks of their personal God.

Oh yes, I know what they say: "It will be well for those who fear God, and show reverence before him; and it will not be well for the wicked, for their days will not lengthen like a shadow simply because they show no reverence before God." But what occurs here on the earth is absurd.

So, on the one hand, you see no evidence of justice being dispensed by a personal God nor do you find, on the other hand, that Nature deals effectively with the problem of evil. Why do you feel so strongly about this?

*I know I have said, **Let not your emotions be quickly aroused, for anger lurks in the bosom of a fool.** But I find it very difficult not to feel angry at what I see. I know that **it is better to judge a matter at its end than at its beginning, and so a patient spirit is better than an arrogant one.** But I simply lose my patience at what I see.*

What is it then that you have seen?

Some righteous people get what the wicked deserve, and some wicked people get what the righteous deserve! This, I say, makes no sense at all.

Are you sure about this? What is your evidence?

In these fleeting days of my life I have seen it all, from a righteous man perishing in spite of his righteousness to a wicked man living long in spite of his evil-doing.

But, if someone's wicked acts result in undeserved prosperity, surely that person will be subjected to strong condemnation from the majority of people so that he will have to suffer at least the shame of ignominy. That in itself would be some form of just punishment. Indeed the prospect of being shamed or ostracised has often proved to be a deterrent against wrongdoing. Have you not found this to be so?

That's not the case at all! Indeed, I have seen wrong-doers buried with pomp and because they frequented the holy place, they were praised in the very city where they did their evil deeds. This also makes no sense.

I see you are convinced that, since the righteous often suffer and the wicked often flourish, we cannot expect to find justice in this world. So while we humans may have a strong moral sense (as you yourself clearly do), this is not the case with the world at large. Nature does not operate with any moral consistency. But this is much the same complaint as we find in the Book of Job, and there it was assumed that the world is controlled by a personal God who is expected to be moral.

I know that book. It was written by a sage who lived before my time.

Then you know that its chief character, Job, was first afflicted by a dreadful illness and then he suffered the loss of his whole family. He believed himself to be innocent of any wrongdoing. So he complained to God that that not only was life unfair, but that God was in fact immoral in allowing it. Job challenged God to defend himself in the open court against the charge of injustice.

Yes, and I recall that several of his friends strongly defended the morality of God, and maintained that Job must have been guilty of some serious misdemeanour even if he was unaware of it. They urged him to confess his sins and seek God's forgiveness.

Quite so, and I assume that although Job was more of a theist than you, you'd nevertheless support him over against the conventional theology of the so-called "comforters." So what is your response to Job's complaint?

Naturally I have great sympathy with Job, and up to a point I support his challenge to God. But I also advise caution and say, **Do not be over-righteous or try to seem over-wise.**

I'm surprised by your response. You seem to be uttering a mild rebuke, both to people like Job and to people like his comforters. Are you implying that Job was so adamant about his righteousness that he became self-righteous?

I do! The comforters, on the other hand, are so committed to their defence of God that they have become blind to reality. In their attempt to defend accepted convention they had become "over-wise."

I take it that you advise a more moderate response, one that's not absolute and final, but always open to review in the light of new evidence. This suggests that you don't expect any easy or clear-cut solutions to our moral problems. Whereas the theistic God supposedly reveals his will in black-and-white terms, Nature seems to work in various shades of grey, leaving us to sort things out the best way we can. Indeed, I get the impression that you are opposed to extremes of any kind, even though they may arise from some worthwhile aspirations and genuine endeavour. Does this correctly sum up your thoughts on the issue?

Yes, I am opposed to extremists, for they are often blind to other points of view and alternative motives. For example, **I saw, then, that all hard work and successful endeavour spring from a man's rivalry with his neighbour. This too is futile, like chasing after the wind.**

So you think that if we go to extremes in our various endeavours, it may reflect some hidden motive on our part. In other words, what often prompts us to exert ourselves to the very limit may be the inner desire to beat our competitors. But surely you wouldn't discourage the genuine endeavour to achieve excellence, for once we give up the attempt to do our best, we may be on the downward path that leads to slothfulness. I'm sure you're aware of the ancient Jewish proverb, "Go to the ant, you sluggard, and be wise."

And it is also said, "The fool folds his arms and destroys himself." But I say, "Better one handful gained with ease than two handfuls gained by hard work and chasing after the wind."

I'm a little puzzled by that. You seem to imply that we should neither be lazy nor work too hard. At first that sounds a little like the "middle way" commended by the Buddhists. In their encounter with the problem of universal suffering, they advise us to avoid setting our expectations too high since failure to reach them only brings further mental stress. But you seem to think excessively hard work is just a waste of effort.

Indeed I do! What comes to people for all the hard work and mental stress their occupation has forced them to endure in this world? For all of their days bring pain and grief; even at night their minds get no rest. This too is futile.

I grant you, of course, that striving too hard in the pursuit of happiness may give rise to grave disappointment, or perhaps even disillusionment. But have we not strayed from our main topic—the question of whether the injustice we see in the world means that life is fundamentally unfair?

I have no doubt that it is for something more I have seen on the earth: at the very seat of justice there is wickedness; in the very place where righteousness should be, there is transgression.

Ecclesiastes, you startle me. That might seem a relatively mild accusation in our world today but it was certainly not so in your day. No wonder you chose to write under a pseudonym, for your critics could easily have construed such a charge as an act of treason and that would have led to dire consequences.

Until rather recently, after all, "the seat of justice" connoted the supreme ruler, usually a king or emperor, and such rulers wielded absolute power. And as history makes clear, it was very dangerous in the past for a subject to question the righteousness of royal decisions. The kings of your own Davidic dynasty were thought to rule by divine right, and the king's word was considered second in authoritative power only to that of God.

But those on the seat of justice should wield the power of life and death. That is just the way it is and has always been. So if the ruling king is good we rejoice; but if he is unjust, all we can do is deplore the fact and take the consequences.

Alas, in some countries, it is still like that today. But for most of us it is rather different. Only a few centuries ago we reached the point of openly challenging royal authority. We even executed some kings who were deemed at the time to be unjust or to have denied their people basic human freedoms. Out of this struggle for power has evolved what we call democracy, a system of government in which ultimate power, and hence the "seat of justice," rests with the people. We now elect our own leaders, challenge them continually, and replace them with others when the majority of people think the time is ripe for change. And thus it is not unusual for modern people to complain of incompetence or even what you refer to as wickedness at the very seat of justice.

But does this democracy you speak of really work? It seems to me unlikely that the majority of people have enough wisdom to share in the responsibility of government.

I concede there are some problems with democracy but it is still preferable to our being dictated to by the powerful few. We have made some progress towards achieving a more egalitarian society, particularly by providing a good education for all. And I'm glad to tell you that over the last century or two we have discarded the notion that some people are destined by God to be rich and powerful and others to be poor, disadvantaged and uneducated. Even Jesus of Nazareth is said to have declared, "The poor you will have with you always," and many traditional Christians took this to be divine warrant for doing nothing to achieve a greater degree of justice.

Further, starting in the last century there has been increasing acceptance of the principle of basic human rights. We have put into place such schemes as the "welfare state" and "social justice." Even so, we still have a long way to go.

Good for you! But what did you find to be the causes of injustice? You may remember I said, **If you witness social oppression of the poor—the denial of justice and human rights—do not be astonished at what goes on!**

Why do you think we might be astonished? Is it because you've found out something about the root causes of injustice that we should know about?

Yes I have! **It's because one bureaucrat is subject to a higher one, and still higher ones lord it over them both.**

In other words, you are telling me that you attribute the oppression of the poor to the structure of society, to the established chains of authority from top to bottom. In that case, I suppose it stands to reason that if what you call the very seat of justice is filled with wickedness and corruption, then a just society is little more than an unrealistic dream—especially if nearly everybody is under the control of someone else. Well, it may be some small satisfaction for you to know that even in democratic countries we often find reason to complain of bureaucratic control.

And remember that land is of value to everybody, so every cultivated field has someone ruling over it.

It's interesting you trace social injustice back to the owner-
ship of land. I know that even in your day peasants were being
displaced from their land and finding themselves at the mercy
of the landed gentry. We shall come back to that later, but
first let's look at the larger problem of one nation invading
another and violating a people's natural sovereignty. Plenty of
that went on in your era with the rise and fall of empires. Alas,
it has continued right up to the present, especially as the nations of Europe colonized the rest of the world to establish
powerful and profitable empires. It is the consistent cry of
indigenous peoples today that they have been dispossessed of
their land by the imperialists and hence deprived of their basic
human rights.

*Quite so; that's one of my primary complaints also, and a cen-
tral reason why I said there is no justice in the world.*

Well, here is a case that will be of special interest to you, as a
Jew. Ever since the destruction of Jerusalem by the Babylonians,
Jews have lived in what they call the Diaspora. This state of
being scattered among the other nations had already started
by the time you were living. (Indeed that fact has made it all
the more difficult for me to discover where you lived when you
wrote.) Jews have not had a country of their own for well over
two thousand years. But about half a century ago a new state of
Israel was established for the Jewish people in their ancestral
land, the place then known as Palestine. Unfortunately, it has
involved the forcible dispossession of many of the previous inhabitants of the land—people we call Palestinians.

*Was it really necessary to establish a Jewish state, especially
if it entailed the displacement of these people you call the
Palestinians?*

For you to understand that I must bring you up to date on
Jewish history. Those Jews who lived within Christendom suffered from continual persecution. This anti-Semitism (as it is

called) became more severe in the nineteenth century and reached a shocking climax when Nazi Germany attempted to annihilate the Jewish people altogether in their death camps. This tragedy became known as the Holocaust.

Yet even before that, a Jewish political movement called Zionism had begun to work towards the establishment of a Jewish state as a way to counter anti-Semitism. What better place to do that than in the very land from which Jews had been forced to emigrate so long ago? Indeed, the Israelis argue that in establishing the state of Israel, they are simply reclaiming the land that God had promised them at the beginning of their history as a people.

I wish I could take you there to see it all for yourself, for I cannot help wondering what you'd make of it. Would you side with the Israelis, who are your blood descendants? Or would you side with the Palestinians who have been dispossessed of their land just as your own ancestors had been in ancient times? It's a very tricky problem!

But I see it as a human problem. You must have noticed I never revealed any great interest in national or ethnic groups. As you correctly said of me, I'm a humanist more than a Jew. We are all humans and must at last learn to treat each other as such. But we don't do a very good job of that, do we? **I saw for myself, as I applied my mind to everything done on the face of the earth, that people lord it over one another to their own hurt.**

So in your view, whether we are kings, emperors, bureaucrats, or merely landowners, we all contribute to social injustice and the oppression of the poor whenever we lord it over others. I suspect you are right in seeing the pursuit of power over others as the root cause of all oppression, and in the end, as you say, it brings suffering to all.

What about turning to the subject of oppression *within* a society? Great numbers of people in modern times have been deeply concerned about the suffering of the oppressed poor;

and none has been more influential than a philosopher named Karl Marx. He too was a Jew, and was initially influenced by a rabbi called Moses Hess. (Doesn't it seem strange that so many of those I have been bringing to your attention were descendents of your people?) Marx appeared at the height of what we call the Industrial Revolution, and he deplored the way that landowners and industrialists sought to increase their wealth and power by grinding the landless poor into the dust.

*I have always said: **Whoever loves money will never be satisfied by amassing it, nor the lover of riches with his income. This shows the futility of seeking wealth.***

Well you may say it! But how is the problem to be overcome? Hess thought the solution lay in the just redistribution of land and of accumulated wealth, but Marx believed that the problem went much deeper than that. In his view, it could not be adequately dealt with by populist programmes that grew out of such slogans as "a fair day's wage for a fair day's work." These, he argued, did not get to the root of the problem. He believed human beings were embroiled in a class struggle between the greedy, exploiting, despotic class he called "My Lord Capital" and the exploited, tormented, enslaved class he named the "Collective Worker."

I suspect Marx saw himself as a modern Moses leading the oppressed out of slavery into a new land of opportunity. He looked to a time when the oppressed poor would rise up against the ruling classes and establish a classless society in which all people would share the land collectively. Clearly, this is much like your understanding that "land is of value to everybody."

Perhaps so, but have I not already made it clear that I am opposed to violent revolutions and to any form of extremism?

Therefore you wouldn't be at all surprised by what actually happened. The social revolution that Marx heralded was so idealistic that it did not come about immediately, as he fervently expected it to. When in the twentieth century, particularly in the countries of Russia and China, attempts were made to establish Marxist states, what resulted was something far from Marx's ideal. Before long the Communist Party became a new ruling class, and the people had simply exchanged one set of rulers for another. Perhaps you can guess what went wrong.

Yes, indeed! You no doubt recall what I said on that subject: **Here is another evil I have seen on the face of the earth: the sort of error that emanates from the ruler. Fools are often appointed to high positions while the rich occupy the lowly ones. I have seen slaves on horseback, while princes go on foot like slaves.**

Yes, that sounds very like the topsy-turvy world that resulted from the revolutions Marx had inspired. In the great land of China, the Communist government of their leader Mao carried out a disastrous cultural revolution in which many members of the educated and skilled elite were sent into the fields to do the tasks of the peasants.

But the kind of thing you refer to happened elsewhere also. In some African countries the indigenous people who replaced the colonising imperialists lacked the expertise required for good government, and as newly found power went to their heads they soon acted like the very despots they had overthrown. If I were to take you on a tour through our world today, you'd perhaps conclude that in spite of our sophistication and our technology—and even allowing for such social progress as we have sometimes made—the poor are often worse off today than they were in your day. And it's all because they have been denied control of the land that supplied their livelihood.

What you tell me suggests that I was correct in seeing injustice as a problem inherent in the human condition. As I said, **see the endless tears of the oppressed for whom no one provides comfort! Since their oppressors wield all the power, no one can ease their suffering.**

Indeed, that succinctly describes the state of the Jews in Nazi-controlled Europe in the middle of the last century. It is also the state of the Palestinians who now suffer at the hands of the Israelis. And it is also the state of the poor and the hungry in what we call the Third World. After World War II we set up the United Nations Organisation, partly as an attempt to prevent further war and partly to tackle shared problems on a global scale. But though it has done a great amount of good and constructive work, it has often been rendered powerless by the powerful nations. No doubt this is a further example of what you so acutely observed: "People lord it over one another to their own hurt." The sad result is that far too little seems to have changed with regard to the poor and oppressed since your times—except that the population explosion has simply increased the scale of the problem.

Clearly we have found no solution to the problems of injustice and oppression that you raised so long ago and that still plague the world. I'm forced to concede that you were correct in your conclusion that for far too many people life is oppressively unfair, while others enjoy more happiness and satisfaction than they can possibly be said to deserve. Why do you think we humans continue to treat one another so badly?

You may think my answer to that to be a simplistic one, but I think it is as true for you as it has been for us: **Human hearts are full of evil. There is madness in people's hearts while they live, and after that they join the dead.**

I find that to be a very bleak judgment of the human condition, yet it does seem that an irrational and largely ineradicable selfishness in each of us contributes to the moral disorder we observe in the world. Nevertheless, I see it balanced by the many unexpected acts of kindness that people do for one another. In the end, it all comes down to the individual actions of individual human beings. *We* are responsible for most of the injustices we observe and only *we* can put them right. As we have seen,

Nature does not reward the righteous and punish the wicked in any consistent way. Inasmuch as Nature therefore seems to be quite amoral, do you think we can discern any hint of purpose in the way things are organized?

To be sure, I long wrestled with that problem, and at last could conclude only that, as I put it, **The aim of Nature with regard to the human race is to test them and to show them that they are but animals.**

I take you to mean that Nature keeps reminding us of our place in the world—that we are not the lords of creation we too often take ourselves to be, but creatures of the earth like all the other animals. To think and act otherwise is to suffer from hubris. And that in turn suggests that when I queried you earlier about your reference to *elohim* being in the sky, you were really saying that the power of Nature always transcends us and we on the earth must submit to it. Strive as we may to create better lives for ourselves and others, we must in the end accept our life on earth and all that comes with it, even when circumstances treat us unfairly. As I recall, you summed it up in a nutshell.

Yes, I did. I assume you are referring to a rather pessimistic—though I would insist realistic—little anecdote of mine. **A dreadful evil I have seen on this earth: hoarded riches that have harmed their owner or have been lost through a bad investment. Then the man fathers a son and has nothing in his hand. As he came forth naked from his mother's womb, so naked he returns to earth, just as he came. Not a thing can he retrieve from his labour, nothing that he can carry away in his hand.**

That is indeed a sad but poignant little tale about the injustice you find in the world. It reminds me of the stories told by Jesus, the sage who came after you and was famous for his parables. We call them by that name because they started with, "The kingdom of God is like this." But your parable, if I may refer to it as such, says in effect, "Life is like this." When someone relates to us a personal story (as you've just done), particularly one that has an unexpected and unfortunate conclusion, we often simply say, "Such is life!"

We, too, find that life is often grossly unfair, of course much more so to some than to others. This is not a moral world; Nature is thoroughly amoral and has no special interest in the livelihood or well-being of us humans. What justice we do observe in the world springs from us humans, and recognizing this can prompt us to care for one another and even extend that concern to some animals.

*That's why I said: **Why die before your time? Far better that you grasp hold of righteousness and not lose your grip on wisdom, for the man who is in awe of Nature will succeed both ways.***

But since we ourselves are part of that Nature you urge us to hold in awe, if we humans act wisely and do the right thing by Nature, it might be said that the once amoral Nature is at last showing signs of becoming moral. Is that what you hinted at when you said we might succeed both ways?

As a matter of fact, we are now coming to see not only that animals, birds and other living things have equal right with us to share the earth's bounties, but also that we humans are more and more becoming responsible for their well-being. Only quite recently have we been alerted to our pressing need to care for the whole earth. Granted, then, that life is often unfair, and it is up to us to take the moral lead on behalf of Nature, how do you suggest that we address the situation?

*With regard to action I urge this: **Everything your hand finds to do, execute with all your might, for in the underworld of the dead to which you are going there is no working, no thinking, no knowledge and no wisdom.***

An underworld of the dead to which we all go? Such an idea would seem to open up all sorts of questions. The subject of death and what follows is one we must discuss next time.

7

IS DEATH THE
END OF US?

Just as we were ending our last discussion, Ecclesiastes, you sprang a surprise on me by referring to the underworld of the dead. Such a place has no reality for us today. I know that in your day it was common for people to believe in an underworld where the dead continue to exist as "shades." The Greeks called it Hades and you Jews called it Sheol. This notion appears to have been widespread in ancient times, at least throughout the area we now call the Middle East. I suspect it had slowly arisen as a result of the practice of burying the dead in the earth.

Job referred to Sheol in his musings about the future, but he summarily dismissed it as a place that could offer any sort of hope for solving the problem of the unfairness of life. The reason was that the underworld, as then imagined, was neither a place of heavenly delights nor one involving any form of punishment. As Job saw it, existence in Sheol was not really life at all; rather it had become simply a euphemism for death. Now that you've mentioned it I would like to find out if you thought as he did. Please refresh my memory on what you actually said last time.

I'm happy to do so. What I said was this: **In the underworld of the dead to which you are going, there is no working, no thinking, no knowledge and no wisdom.**

No thinking! No knowledge! That certainly is not life as we experience it in this world. I assume that when you say the dead who exist there have no knowledge, you are asserting they don't experience any awareness or what we call consciousness.

Consciousness is a new concept to me but I suspect that it refers to what I had in mind when I said, **living people at least know that they will die, while the dead know absolutely nothing.**

And that means the dead cannot be aware of any feelings of satisfaction or regret about the kind of life they have lived. As you understand it, then, Sheol is a place where the dead have no conscious relationship, let alone verbal intercourse, with one another. Rather, it's where the dead enter into a deep and permanent sleep.

Nor do they have any hope for further reward.

So they no longer have any awareness of what they have done in life, whether good or bad, nor any memory of who they once were, nor any sense of the future.

And even the memory of them is soon lost. Their loves, their hates and their jealousies have already perished. Never again will they take part in anything that happens on the face of the earth.

It appears to me that the underworld of Sheol was simply a name for the state of oblivion into which the dead pass, eventually to be forgotten completely by the living. That's tantamount to saying that death brings each of us to an absolute end. So how does that square with the way you Jews thought of a living person as a physical body into which God had breathed his breath of life? I understand that some Jewish sages suggested that, although at death the body turns to dust in the earth, the breath that gave life to the body returns to the God who gave it. Do you believe that too?

I don't know what to believe. **Who knows whether mankind's breath of life rises upward to the heavens and the animals' breath of life descends downward to the earth?**

On that question, at least, you are adopting what we call an agnostic position. In other words you don't profess to know exactly what happens to whatever in us gives us life. On the other hand, you seem absolutely certain that in the underworld of the dead there is no knowledge or consciousness of our identity. The dead have simply ceased to exist in any real way at all. What has led you to this conviction?

I have observed it for myself. **For what happens to humans is what happens to animals; they share the same fate. As the one dies, so does the other; the one breath of life is the same for them all.**

So although you are a Jew, you evidently don't believe what the Torah says in its very first chapter—"God created humankind in his own image." Those words express, among other things, the conviction (still held by many people today) that we humans are quite different from all the other animals and, presumably, are intended for a different destiny. Some have even thought of themselves as half-animal, half-angel. But you seem quite adamant that we humans are so truly animal in every way that we must share the same fate of oblivion. Since today's science of zoology has led us to the same conclusion, you were well ahead of your time in reaching that insight. How did you come to it?

As you know, I pride myself on reaching my convictions on the basis of what I have observed in life. By studying the life cycles of animals and humans **I myself have come to know that the same fate overtakes them both.**

You remind me of our great philosopher David Hume. He observed that humans grow from infancy through maturity to old age in much the same way as animals do; and then, like the animals, they show signs of decay before they die. He greatly upset the people of his time by concluding from this that there is no after-life for humans any more than there is for animals.

I entirely agree with your philosopher. **Humans have no advantage over the animals. For nothing they do has any lasting significance. All go to the same place; all come from dust, and to dust all return.**

But if, like the animals, we all return to dust, and death brings our conscious existence to an end forever, it must mean that those who suffer oppression and evil in this world have lost all chance of having their wrongs put right. Will they never be vindicated? Is there no consolation for them?

None at all! That's precisely the root of my complaint. Indeed, I would go further and say that because of the injustice they have suffered in the world, **I consider the dead (since they have met death already) more fortunate than the living (who are alive to this day).**

By making that despairing comment you remind me again of Job, for at one point in his soliloquy over his suffering, he expressed the wish that he had perished on the day he was born. He was coming to the conclusion that this is such a cruel and unjust world that we are better off never to have been born.

I agree with that too. As I have said, **more fortunate than both the living and the dead is the one who has never existed, for he has not seen the evil that occurs on the earth.**

Isn't that altogether too gloomy a conclusion? Certainly those who have never existed have never suffered and have had no experience of evil but they have had no experience of anything! Surely it's better to have had the experience of life, even if it involves suffering or disappointment, than to have had no experience at all. Why do you feel so pessimistic about life?

I came to hate life, because whatever happens in this world causes me distress. Everything is as futile as chasing after the wind.

On that point I cannot agree with you at all. I concede that life can bring distress, but not all of life is like that. Because of the injustices and incredible cruelty that some people suffer (phenomena you rightly deplore) you seem to forget altogether the great enjoyment that people can also experience in life. In any case, even in our distress we may still look into the future with hope. We have a saying, "Hope springs eternal in the human heart."

*Thank you for that rebuke! I agree that I went too far and now concede that **whoever is still in the company of the living has some hope; even a dog, if it is alive, is better off than a dead lion!***

I'm relieved to hear you say that, for you were giving me the impression you believe that death and non-existence are preferable to life. I can see that you are still struggling with the same problem as Job was and are distressed at finding no solution to it. I concede that when a friend dies from a terminal illness that has brought much pain, we sometimes say that death has come as a welcome release. But that's very different from despairing of life itself.

By far the majority of people who suffer injustice in life still cling desperately to life and justifiably so. They retain at least a glimmer of hope that there may be something better to come. Accounts seem to indicate that during the Nazi Holocaust that I mentioned to you earlier, those Jews who never lost hope had a better chance of survival than those who gave into despair.

So I'm glad you agree that, except in extreme circumstances, life is better than death. I believe that when disaster strikes us we should do our best to pick ourselves up and move on, rather than allowing ourselves to be completely overwhelmed by the evil in the world. I've noticed quite recently in our society today how people who have suffered some unexpected loss or disaster so often say they want to "put it behind them and move on."

*I'm returning to such a thought myself. **I have come to realise that nothing is better for people than to be happy and to do good while they live.***

Ah, now that's more like it! But I have sensed in your words that, besides sharing Job's concern about undeserved suffering, you are greatly disturbed about something else. Can you tell me what it is?

This is my problem: life seems all too perplexing and short.
Who knows what makes for a good life? Our days are few
and fleeting, and we are like shadows passing through them.
Life is beyond our understanding, and seems to be over almost
immediately after it has begun.

If it's the shortness of human life that worries you, you have plenty of company! Certainly it is tragic when death strikes the young, and I suppose child mortality was even more common in your day than in ours; though even today, in what we call the third-world countries, the lives of far too many children are very short—and often full of suffering at that.

But people who at least reach middle age, and even more those who go on to dignified old age, surely have much in life to rejoice about. You clearly reached the years of maturity. Didn't you experience some joy in doing so, even to the point of feeling some satisfaction in your achievements?

No, I did not. **I turned about and fell into despair at the**
thought of all my futile labour in this world.

But why do you think your labour has been futile? After all, you've just agreed that, instead of allowing ourselves to be weighed down by the amount of evil and injustice we find in the world, it's better for us to use what life we have to be happy and do some good. Is it because your eventual death deprived you of the fruit of your labours that you regard them as futile? How does it do that?

Surely you recall what I said: **It can happen that a man**
works hard, displaying wisdom, knowledge, and skill, and
yet have to leave his resulting assets to a man who has not
laboured for them at all. This is not only meaningless, but ut-
terly wrong.

I don't agree and I feel your judgment is too individualistic. In this matter the new idea of evolution may help you. I invite you to think of all that you received from the many generations that went before you, including such basic things as the language you learned from your parents and the culture into which you were born. It is only because of what we have inherited from our countless forebears from primitive times onwards that we have been able to develop into the humans we are. Though none of us live to enjoy our achievements forever, those who succeed us will benefit from at least some of what we have said and done. Just think of the way we are being enlightened and stimulated by your words after all this time.

True! Since I knew nothing of the evolution of human culture until you told me, I was not able to think of it that way. But I still deplore the phenomenon of death.

I suspected that was your problem, as it was for so many people in your day. People used to speak of the "sting of death" and of the grave gaining the final victory. Death was thought of as the chief enemy of life, and treated as something to be held at bay as long as possible. We still often think like that. Death comes as an unwelcome and often unexpected intrusion into life, up-setting our plans and frustrating our endeavours. Even worse, it brings to a sudden stop the loving relationships we have with other people, which are so important for an enjoyable and ful-filling life. It is perfectly understandable, therefore, that we so often think of death in purely negative terms.

Exactly. How can death be anything else but negative? What good ever comes out of death?

Surprisingly, a great deal. Let me remind you that even you said a little while ago that death is preferable to a life of continuous suffering. But when we consider the wider implications of the phenomenon of death, we find that it plays a crucial role in the evolution of life; indeed it made the evolution of species pos-sible. Thus, we humans evolved to be what we are today because of the deaths of the countless generations of our pre-human ancestors who preceded us. Life and death belong together; we cannot have one without the other. Death is an essential ele-ment of the conditions that Nature has imposed upon life. To experience the enjoyment of life we must also accept that each life will come to an end in death.

But doesn't death destroy any meaning or purpose that the life of each particular person might have? My protest about life, as I said before, is that it is "short-lived," "fast-fleeting." "Everything is empty of any lasting significance!"

What I understand from this is that—as I suspected—your distress about the injustice in the world that we discussed in our last encounter was exacerbated by the shortness of life and the inevitability of death. That's why these opening words of your book have been your continual theme song. But now I wish to tell you that your protest against the apparent meaninglessness of life did not go unanswered; people began to wonder about the possibility of what they called eternal life. Such a concept not only addressed the shortness of life but was thought to provide life with "lasting significance."

I must now sketch for you the story of how the idea of eternal life developed over the next two millennia. Please be patient with me, for this will take some time.

I'm very curious to hear the story for I cannot imagine how anything can possibly reverse the finality of death and so provide lasting significance to life.

What sparked this story in the first place was the problem of undeserved suffering that so gripped Job and yourself. And although at first it led Job to wish he'd never been born, he said something rather different later on in his soliloquy. He expressed the hope that after his death a champion would arise in his defence and prove his innocence to God. Then Job even dared to hope that somehow, in spirit if not in flesh, he would hear of his vindication from God himself.

To be sure, that novel thought was actually written before your lifetime and, if you ever read it, you must have dismissed it as wishful thinking. But a century or so after you, some devout Jews known as Pharisees took Job's desperate cry for help a stage further. Although they continued to accept death as the end of conscious existence, they came to believe that since the world had a beginning it would also have an end—and that when that end comes there will be a Final Judgment. At that point in the future all who have ever lived will be resurrected from their graves and brought before the throne of God to hear the divine pronouncement on the kind of life they had lived. Those who receive the verdict of divine approval will proceed to everlasting life, while those who do not will be condemned to shame and everlasting contempt.

I have never heard of such an idea among Jewish people and it sounds rather preposterous to me. I know our prophet Ezekiel referred to the resurrection of the Jewish people from the valley of dry bones, but it's quite clear that he was speaking symbolically.

Many of today's scholars think this idea of a general resurrection followed by a Last Judgment actually originated with the Zoroastrians of Persia and began to enter Jewish thinking towards the end of the period of Persian supremacy. It's not surprising that when the notion first took root in Jewish culture it was strongly rejected by traditional Jews such as the Sadducees. They not only thought it unbelievable, just as you did when I mentioned it to you; they even made fun of it.

Nevertheless, it finally came to be widely adopted, first by Jews and later by the two great religions of Christianity and Islam that drew so much from Jewish thought and practices. I suspect the idea of the Last Judgment won a place in people's imaginations because it met a deep spiritual need. It opened a door of hope to those who, like Job, felt crushed by injustice and unjustified suffering. It had the effect of reassuring people that this is a moral universe after all, one in which justice is finally meted out to everybody. In addition, it gave hope to people that death, this so-called enemy of humankind, would be finally conquered.

But surely this unbelievable notion is just wishful thinking.
What is the evidence for it? **Who can tell humankind what**
will happen in the world after we are gone?

True, the Last Judgment is imagined as being in the unknown
future, and so it lies beyond proof or disproof of any kind. And
you, I know, understandably insisted on basing your convictions
on what you could observe for yourself. So you may well wonder
why people came to believe it at all.

In its Zoroastrian origins the belief no doubt spread because
of the authority of the prophet Zoroaster. But why did Jews
believe it? I suggest that the reason lies in the desperate nature
of later Jewish experience. The Book of Daniel, the Jewish writing in which the idea first appears, was composed during the
Maccabaean wars, when the Jews revolted against a Syrian ruler
who was bent on stamping out their culture by destroying their
synagogues and Holy Scriptures. It appears that many loyal
and devout Jews adopted this new hope and clung firmly to it,
believing that their God Yahweh would surely mete out justice
to the young Jewish soldiers who in effect became martyrs to
their faith.

Not only would this odd notion have been quite foreign to Jews
of my day, but it also lacks any rational foundation. I can see
how some of my Jewish successors may have turned to it out of
desperation, but why did it spread to the Christians you told
me about?

What happened was that the spread of the Roman Empire
during the next few centuries caused the Jewish people such
suffering and uncertainty that many thought the end of the
world was at hand. It was in these eschatological times (as we
now call them) that a new Jewish sect grew up around Jesus of
Nazareth, the Jewish sage whom I mentioned to you earlier. He
was not so much the founder of Christianity as its foundation,
for he came to be worshipped as a divine figure who would save

his followers from the cataclysmic destruction they believed to be imminent.

It was largely under the inspiration of another Jew (later known as St. Paul) that this Jewish sect burst out into the Gentile world and developed into the new world religion of Christianity. That's how the idea of the Last Judgment, though originally held by only a few Jews and Jewish Christians, began to spread. At first, all the Christians who followed Paul's teaching believed the end of the world was imminent, and Paul went so far as to claim that it would occur during his own lifetime.

But I must again protest: **Who can tell us what will happen in this world after we are gone?**

I know this must puzzle you, but the Christians believed that God had given them empirical evidence of the resurrection yet to come. Indeed, shortly after the Romans had executed this man Jesus (evidently because they saw him as a threat to their rule), the story arose that he had risen from the dead. Then Paul had an experience on the road to Damascus that convinced him he had personally encountered this risen Jesus, and soon began preaching the resurrection of Jesus as the beginning of the general resurrection—the first fruits, he said, of the resurrection to come. So Paul really believed he had empirical evidence (the kind you are always seeking) of the general resurrection that was shortly to occur. And though the Greeks simply laughed at Paul when he spoke about it in Athens, his fellow Christians deemed his personal convictions to be quite sufficient evidence for them.

Another factor that may help you to understand why Christians became convinced about the general resurrection and Final Judgment was a series of Roman persecutions on an even larger scale than the persecution of the Jews in Maccabaean times. Indeed, to offer encouragement to those suffering persecution, a man known as St. John the Divine wrote a rather strange book called Revelation, in which he claimed to have had a vision of how it would all end.

*My natural scepticism makes me suspicious of all who claim to have visions of the future. **After all, who can enable them to peer into what will happen after them?***

Yes, you have a valid point. And as a matter of fact, because the end of the world did not arrive as expected, but was soon felt to be further away than ever, a strange, unexpected and very interesting development took place in Christian thought. Because Christianity was spreading primarily in Greek culture, an idea borrowed from the Greeks entered the collective Christian imagination.

The great Greek philosopher Plato had expounded a view of the human condition that was very different from the one held by you Jews. He taught that the real essence of each person is a spiritual entity he called a soul. The soul contains our memory and the knowledge accumulated during life; it is immortal and hence survives the death of the body. For those who espouse this belief, then, death is not as complete and final as you took it to be.

I find this idea of an immortal soul a very strange one. Is it not obvious that we humans are bodies, made alive by breath? We Jews call a living person a nephesh. As I said before, I don't profess to know what happens to that breath when it leaves the body for the last time, but surely it is nothing like this immortal soul that Plato imagined.

True! You and Plato understood the human condition quite differently. You regarded a person as a body enlivened by the air it breathed, and even used the same word for air, breath and spirit. But Plato did not think of us humans as bodies, but as eternal souls who are temporarily resident, almost imprisoned, in a body of flesh. It was Plato's influence among others that led Christians to adopt a negative attitude towards the human body, even coming to see the flesh as an enemy of the soul, whereas you Jews viewed the human body more positively, and quite rightly so.

Since the Christian Church was developing within Greek culture, it rather naturally adopted Plato's idea of the soul as a way of solving the problem of the ever-receding end of the world. And by combining Platonism with the belief in a Final Judgment, it taught that our souls face judgment as soon as we die.

But what happened to the idea of the Judgment of the whole world at the end of time?

That was already such a permanent part of Christian teaching that it also had to be retained; the result was that Christians came to believe in two Judgments. First would be the judgment of the soul at the point of death; then, at the world's end, the soul is to be rejoined with the resurrected body and a second but final Judgment would take place.

I find that not only unbelievable but unnecessarily complicated.

At first many Christians did too, and they resisted this change. That's shown by the fact that the earliest Christian epitaph was retained for a very long time. It was R.I.P., short for *Requiescat in Pace*, meaning in effect "Let him or her rest here in the grave in peace until the resurrection." Eventually, however, this new understanding of the human condition—namely that we are immortal souls temporarily inhabiting physical bodies—almost completely replaced what Christianity had inherited from your Jewish culture.

As a result, the Final Judgment at the end of time became marginalized and virtually forgotten. Thus the Christian view of the world and of human destiny eventually became quite different from what it had been at the beginning. Instead of being the way to be saved from the imminent destruction of the world (as it was at first), and instead of being the way to be saved from the fires of hell (as it was in the Middle Ages), by modern times Christianity had virtually become the way to conquer death.

A well-known Christmas carol written in the mid-eighteenth century to celebrate the birth of the Saviour says it succinctly: "born that man no more may die."

So death was no longer something to be deplored in the way I do? If this soul you talk about simply lives forever, then death has not only lost its sting. It has lost its reality!

Quite so, and that's just how many in our day have come to think about death. They even liken it to a veil that we pass through to another life. Of course the conservative Christians still fear death, though not because it means the end of life, but because of the judgment they expect to face. They believe the righteous will inherit the heavenly realm (or sky above) where God and his angels dwell, while the wicked will be despatched to a fiery place of punishment under the earth called hell.

If hell is conceived to be under the earth, it sounds rather like the underworld of the dead that we call Sheol.

True! Hell was at first seen as a revamped version of Sheol or Hades, so much so that the latter term was sometimes used in its stead. But hell was a place of eternal punishment, not a euphemism for non-existence, as it was for you. Heaven and hell existed in Christian imagination as places that demonstrated the moral meaningfulness of life. They were the Christian answer to your protest about the meaninglessness of life. By the Middle Ages, Christians found this answer so convincing that the places known as heaven and hell, being eternal, seemed even more real than the earth itself.

So thank you, Ecclesiastes, for your patient attention while I sketched this long story for you. But I know what you're going to say, for you've said it several times already.

Indeed, I have. And I shall say it yet again and again: **Who can tell us what will happen in this world after we are gone?**

Exactly, and I must agree with you. But, if you were to ask people why they are so sure of their belief in the "after-life," most Christians would simply answer, "It's the teaching of the church!" or "It's in the Bible." In other words, for many centuries this imaginative picture of human destiny was held to be true because it was understood to have been divinely revealed to the prophets and apostles of old.

If people treat this Bible you speak of as if it were infallible and beyond all questioning they are surely treating it as an idol. As you must know, we Jews regard idolatry is one of the most heinous of sins.

Very true! And it is only during the last three centuries that the rise of empirical science has eroded the very notion of divine revelation by providing a more reliable means of assembling knowledge. Many of us now no longer look to the Bible for the way we are to view the universe or understand the human condition. With the advent of the modern secular world the spiritual domains of heaven and hell have simply dissolved into unreality—another example of your favourite term *hevel.*

Of course many traditionalists flatly reject much modern knowledge, and still hope to enter a heaven where they will be re-united with their loved ones. Others speak vaguely of an "after-life," being very reluctant to surrender all hope of something beyond the grave. After all, when dealing with the death of loved ones, we find it very difficult to accept that they no longer exist; it is much easier to feel that they continue to be what they have always been but in some unseen spiritual realm.

A growing number, however, now accept the finiteness of life, and the finality of death, just as you do. This is demonstrated by the significant change that has taken place in funeral ceremonies. Until a century ago the dead were always buried with a ritual in which they were despatched to the next world with the words, "in the sure and certain hope of the resurrection." Today, more often than not, the dead are cremated, after a ceremony in which the mourners express their gratitude for the life that has just come to an end.

It seems to me that, by accepting death as real and final just as I do, you have come to accept the truth of my words.

Indeed many do just that! Let me illustrate this by quoting you something from the autobiography of one of our well-known writers, Leonard Woolf, who like you was a Jew.

> I have lived my life on the assumption that sooner or later
> I shall pass by annihilation into the same state of non-
> existence from which I suddenly emerged many years ago.
> This passage from non-existence to non-existence seems to
> me a strange and, on the whole, an enjoyable existence. But
> I resent the fact that, as it seems to be practically certain, I
> shall be as non-existent after my death as I was before my
> birth. Nothing can be done about it and I cannot truthfully
> say that my future extinction causes me much fear or pain,
> but I should like to record my protest against it and against
> the universe which enacts it.

That man is a Jew after my own heart. I'm gratified to learn that he has continued to protest against the fact that we are born only to die. So why did you tell me that fantastic story of how people came to believe in a spiritual world inhabited by souls?

I wanted you to understand why, after more than two millennia, much of what you said then seems so strangely relevant to our time. I concede that the complex spiritual world that Christians came to believe in was very inspirational and for a long time seemed quite convincing and comforting, but it existed only in Christian imagination. Its current dissolution makes it appear as a strange interlude that has led us in a circle back to where you were. Your sober and realistic acknowledgement of the finiteness of human life and the finality of death is what we all have to face up to today. Moreover the dissolution of all hope of another life beyond this one has not been all loss, though many still grieve it as such. It may even turn out to be a positive gain.

How can that be so? First you tell me that death need not be judged negatively and now you say there is a positive value to be gained by the loss of all hope beyond death.

An immediate positive consequence of surrendering all hope of a life beyond death is that it would bring an end to a new evil practice that has arisen, that of suicide bombers. Numbers of fanatically devout Muslims willingly sacrifice their own lives in what they (perhaps even justifiably) judge to be a righteous cause. They even kill innocent people believing that as martyrs they will immediately be transported into a heavenly place of bliss when they die. This unfortunately is the kind of practice that can arise when people become over-confident about entering a better existence after death.

As I see it, that's not only an evil practice but also a futile one. Surely life is short enough already without deliberately making it even shorter.

Exactly! But another and more widespread positive consequence of acknowledging this life to be the only one we shall live is that it motivates us to value life all the more and to live it as fully as possible. Further, it encourages us to set more value on the lives of other people as well. It is one reason, for example, why many countries in the post-Christian world now refuse to inflict the death penalty on criminals.

Thus, ironical though it may seem, the phenomenon of death serves an important moral purpose. The realisation that human life is strictly limited in length, and does not go on endlessly forever, has the effect of causing us to give more attention to the way we live it.

*While I continue to deplore the fact of death, I can agree with you that life should be lived to the full. **Therefore I commend the pursuit of happiness. There is nothing better for a man to do in this world than to eat and drink and be happy. Then joy will accompany him in his work for all the days of the life Nature has given him in this world.***

This final bit of advice from you is more encouraging than I expected in view of your earlier remarks. Perhaps this would be a good place for us to stop for now.

8

CHANCE OR
PURPOSE?

We ended our last encounter, Ecclesiastes, on quite a happy note. Though you continue to lament that we humans all come to an end in death, you nevertheless recommend that we should make the most of the life we are given, short-lived though it may be. With this I thoroughly agree.

*Yes, that's it in a nutshell. It's for that very reason that **I saw** **that there is nothing better for people than to be happy in** **their work, because that is their appointed lot.***

I notice you say "appointed lot" rather than, perhaps, "chosen profession or trade." Does that mean you think each of us is intended for a particular life task? Or are you implying that the day of our death is already fixed beforehand in the belief that we are each allotted a specific term to live?

*I was not referring to our life work or to the day of our death, but to the nature of our humanity. **The human condition is** **already known, and a person cannot contend against a power** **mightier than himself.** God (or Nature as you've taught me to say) has made us the way we are with all of our limitations and we must accept that fact and learn to live within those limits.*

That makes you sound rather like what we call an existential-ist—someone who points out that since we didn't choose to be born, it's as if we have been "thrown into existence" and must simply make the most of it. We find it's only after we have been living for some years, and achieved some maturity, that we develop sufficient mental skill to enable us to ask why.

*I like that phrase "thrown into existence." I have often myself felt that **whatever has come to be was already predestined.***

But the word "predestined" makes you sound more like a determinist, and I believe we agreed earlier that you were not. I assume, then, that you're referring to the fact that we are born into a universe that has evolved to be the way it is without our having anything to do with it. And to be sure, the human condition is given to us at birth; to a large degree, we are already shaped, but that includes our capacity to make choices. And though those choices are limited by Nature, we can, to some degree at least, claim an open future in which we are free to decide what sort of life we wish to live.

*That's all very well but **for that matter, who knows what makes for a good life? Our days are few and fleeting, and we are like shadows passing through them.***

You seem to hint that because life is so short it is hardly worthwhile even asking the question of how to live life to the full. Not only can I not agree with that, but I wonder why you've come to take such a negative view about life. Is there something in your past experience that has led you to hold such a despairing outlook?

I hated all the wealth for which I had toiled under the sun, wealth I must leave to the man who succeeds me—for who knows whether he will be prudent or a fool? Yet it is he who will control the fruits of my labour and everything in which I have shown some skill in this world. This is simply meaningless.

So you amassed quite a bit of wealth during your lifetime! Then subsequently you became concerned about what would happen to it. That in itself is no sufficient reason for feeling disillusioned with life. Even though you'll lose all control over it when you die, should you not be grateful that you've done so well and have been able to enjoy the fruits of your labour at least for a time? Let me remind you that in our last discussion you acknowledged that we bring nothing into this world and we take nothing out of it. Since this is just a fact of life, can it be such a disaster that it makes life meaningless?

Indeed it is! It shows that all of our efforts and achievements come to nothing in the end. That's exactly why **I turned back and again saw the futility of this life.**

You keep insisting on the futility of all of our achievements because none of them lasts forever. But isn't it sufficient to enjoy them while we still have them? You yourself often say that we have nothing better to do than eat, drink and be happy in our work. If that's true, then what is the source of your deep discontent? Can you describe it further?

This is how I see it. **Here is a man all alone. He has neither son nor brother, nor can see any end to his hard work, and his eyes are never satisfied with his riches. But he never asks himself, "For whom am I toiling, and depriving myself of good things?"**

That sounds like another of the little parables you tell to illustrate what life is like. Jesus told one rather similar:

> There was a rich person who had a great deal of money, who said, "I shall invest my money so that I may sow, reap and fill my storehouses with produce, that I may lack nothing." This is what he thought in his heart but that very night he died.

Now whereas Jesus was warning his listeners of the uncertainty of life and of how our best laid plans can be overturned by unexpected chance events, you tell us of a person who never pauses to ask himself why he works so hard. You are drawing the attention of your readers to the futility of the unexamined life. Both parables, I should say, point to a deeper question—what is life for? You keep raising the question of whether life has any meaning, but for the most part you seem to conclude that there is none.

That makes you sound even more like the modern existentialists I mentioned earlier. They keep wrestling with such questions as whether life has any purpose, and whether a reason for human existence itself can be discovered. They conclude that this universe is an absurd and meaningless cosmos rather than one in which human suffering has to be attributed to an omnipotent and punitive God. They call upon people to create their own meaning in life in the full awareness that there is no power in the universe that has already prescribed a meaning for them.

Whether you're correct in labelling me an existentialist I don't know, but I do know that **to all of this I directed my full attention, seeking an explanation for it all.** *For example,* **people say that the righteous, the wise and all their deeds are in God's hands; but I say—whether things stem from love or hatred, not a single person will ever know.**

You're right to question whether God takes any special care of the righteous, for the God whom theists claim to believe in seems sometimes to love and at other times to hate. But if we think of God as Nature (as you seem to do), then it becomes clear why no one will ever know whether "things stem from love or hatred." It is simply because Nature neither loves nor hates anyone. Nature brought us into being and Nature takes us away in death. But Nature does not pursue any discernible purpose. There *is* no goal towards which Nature is moving. Consequently it has no special interest in us humans, either as individuals or even as a species.

Further, it is not only the righteous, but all of us who are in the hands of Nature. That's a truth that we humans are painfully having to relearn during this twenty-first century. The very future of the human species has come to depend on how well we understand and learn to live in accordance with the parameters set by Nature.

Indeed some of our modern prophets are sketching dire scenarios for our future, precisely because we have failed to understand and conform to the ways of Nature. In this new global age that we've entered, all nations and peoples will be affected by our actions, and Nature will grant none of us special treatment. It will make no difference whether we are theists or atheists, Christians or Muslims, black or white, rich or poor.

As I see it however **everything they encounter is meaningless because one Fate comes to everybody—to the righteous and to the wicked, to the good, the pure and the unclean, to those who worship and to those who do not. As it is with the good man, so it is with the evil-doer; as with him who swears an oath, so with the one afraid to swear. This is what is wrong with everything that happens in this world. The same fate comes to all.**

Of course death comes to us all and, indeed, is the only certainty in life. But does the inevitability of death render meaningless everything that we do in our lives? Let me offer you as a parable of my own, the example of a man who spent his last years thinking mainly about your words.

His name was Colin McCahon. He is often judged to have been New Zealand's greatest artist, and his works now sell for millions of dollars. But this was not so during his working life. Indeed, he suffered bitter criticism from many in the art world and he remained poor to the end. Eventually he became much gripped by your words and ended his career by simply painting them—in his own distinctive way, of course. He evidently believed that your words expressed just what he felt. Do you recall saying something about a laughing stock?

*Yes I do. I remember that I wrote—***Why make yourself a laughing-stock? Do not be over-wicked and do not prove yourself a fool. Why die before your time?**

Those are some of the very words McCahon chose to paint, evidently feeling that they, along with many other words of yours, were strikingly relevant to our time, and to his own situation in particular. Some of his fellow artists had poked fun at some of his early paintings and one gallery even refused to hang them. McCahon felt he was not understood even though he gave himself passionately to the art to which he was committed. Sadly, he died as an alcoholic, and "before his time." He had been very disappointed by his apparent rejection, yet after his death he became highly honoured and internationally famous.

This is utterly senseless. What a pitiful state of affairs.

True. Still, as you keep reminding me, such is life. It often doesn't seem to make sense. But here comes the point of my story. McCahon's last two years of painting were devoted almost exclusively to putting your words on canvas. Your words spoke to him so pertinently that he was instrumental in bringing them to the attention of people who otherwise would never have heard of them. Is that not one of the great ironies of life that was quite impossible for you to foresee? Your very complaint that nothing lasts not only spoke to him, but had the effect of giving your words a new lease of life.

I'm not so impressed by that fact as you may think. Of course I did not expect my words to last, and am greatly surprised to hear that they are still being read. However, it is not the words themselves that really matter but what they are searching for—and often finding it difficult to convey. Answers to the most important questions about life and death seem always to elude us. **The more words a person uses, the more futile it becomes! So how does that profit anyone?**

Let me suggest that the value may be in the ongoing search itself, rather in finding the final answers. Is it not because there is much in the world that is unknown and mysterious that we find life to be so interesting and exciting? I find it is the search for answers to our questions that gives spice to life. The whole scientific enterprise of modern times has been spurred on by sheer curiosity.

But isn't it futile to keep on looking for something that may not even be there? And are there not some things that may be forever unknowable?

Possibly so! And that may become clearer in the course of the search. For example, the medieval alchemists spent a lot of their time looking for a method of turning base metals into gold. Now we know why that was a waste of time and energy; but this new knowledge then enabled scientists to turn their attention to more profitable pursuits. We often find that the solving of one mystery uncovers a further one, or that while looking for one answer we discover something totally unanticipated. So the more we know, the more we realise what we do not know. This should not discourage us, however, or make us feel that the pursuit of knowledge is futile.

*That may be so, but **I have seen something else in this world. The race is not guaranteed to the swift nor the battle to the strong.** What makes you think your search will be successful?*

Certainly there is no guarantee that our efforts to unfold the secrets of the universe will produce results; but our natural curiosity, if nothing else, keeps motivating us to carry on. Sometimes it's not even persistence but sheer chance that produces results, as with the serendipitous discovery of one of our modern wonder medicines, penicillin.

*That's what I also began to observe. **Food does not necessarily come to the wise, nor wealth to the intelligent, nor favour to the learned; for all alike are subject to time and chance.***

I'm extremely interested to hear you refer to chance. That's something we have become much more aware of in recent times. In ancient days the phenomenon of chance was not sufficiently acknowledged because every event was thought to result from some purpose, however hidden. It was assumed that whatever had not been caused by us humans must have been willed by the gods or by God. Thus we humans became convinced that everything happened for a purpose even though we might not know what that purpose was. Theists still believe that.

It's not surprising, then, that one of the first people to deny the existence of purpose in the non-human universe was the modern prophet, Friedrich Nietzsche, the same man who declared that the God of theism is dead. He said the very concept of purpose is a human creation and we unconsciously project it on to everything we observe in the world. I hope this helps you to understand how far ahead of your time you were when you raised the issue of chance.

*But all that I said was that **all alike are subject to time and chance.***

And you did not realise what an insightful observation that was. You were the only Jew I know of who said anything like it at that time. Indeed, your use of the Hebrew word for "chance" is almost the only time it is found in the whole Bible. Admittedly, the great Greek philosopher Democritus, who lived about two centuries before you, had said, "Everything existing in the universe is the fruit of chance and necessity." Generally speaking, however, people paid little attention to what he and you said about the role of chance, and those insights became lost to view until modern times, as shown by the minor furore that followed the publication in 1971 of a book by the scientist, Jacques Monod, entitled *Chance and Necessity.*

But what did he mean by "necessity"—and why did his book arouse such opposition?

By the term "necessity" Monod was referring to the operation of cause and effect that takes place in what we call the laws of nature. These operate because of the inherent nature of the physical world and not because some outside force such as an all-powerful heavenly being is pulling the strings. A good example is the law of gravity, by which we are able to predict the tides and movements of the heavenly bodies.

Monod was a molecular biologist who argued that while people generally accept the modern scientific discovery of the laws of nature, we are slow to reject the outdated notion that the world was designed and created by an external power called God. He insisted that the universe is becoming increasingly self-explanatory as we come to recognize the interaction of two phenomena—the laws of nature (necessity) and the unpredictability of some events (chance). And the latter, he argued, has been particularly important in the biological evolution of planetary species, including the human race—all of which has taken place as the result of a multitude of chance events, and not because an external supernatural force has been at work in a purposeful way. Such an assertion understandably offended all those people (including, of course, the theists) who assumed there is a purpose behind everything.

That does not surprise me for I myself find your argument hard to follow. Is there any way I can observe for myself the evidence for his claims?

We non-scientists can most easily understand the important role of chance if we simply consider how each of us came into being. First, it was a collection of chance events that brought our parents together, and if they had not met we would not be here at all.

Further, the kind of person we become is partly determined by our genes, though this is something that was quite unknown in your day. This is where necessity operates. However, our conception resulted from a chance event in our mother's womb; it occurred when one particular sperm out of the thousands donated by our father successfully combined with the ovum released that month from our mother's store of eggs. This chance event determined our own unique set of genes that we now call our DNA, a highly complex chemical pattern that distinguishes us from all other humans, including even our siblings.

Of course I know nothing of that, for the knowledge accumulated by your scientists is vastly superior to any that I have had access to. I based my comment about chance on a much simpler and more mundane series of events. For example, I observed that **as fish are caught in a cruel net or birds taken in a snare, so people can be trapped by a moment of misfortune that suddenly overtakes them.**

You call it misfortune but that's just another name for chance. Accidents are a particular variety of chance. Though some accidents can be attributed to carelessness, many occur by what we call pure chance. That's when we often say, "So-and-so just happened to be in the wrong place at the wrong time." Though it was such occurrences that made you aware of the frequency of chance events, that fact in no way detracts from the insightfulness of your remark.

What modern science has done is to show that your observation was simply the tip of a great iceberg. Charles Darwin explained that while the evolution of species by natural selection is the consequence of certain conditions of nature, the process also requires the occurrence of random chance mutations.

You cannot expect me to understand that. Your scientists are clearly operating in a world of thought that's far beyond me.

And beyond me also, for today's leading physicists are making discoveries that most of us struggle to understand. Take, for example, what they call quantum physics, the study of energy in its infinitesimal form (energy is the basic substance of which all material objects are formed). It has been found that when energy is reduced to its smallest possible quantity (quantum), its behaviour becomes impossible to predict—or to put it another way, at the very heart of matter is the element of chance. When this quantum theory was being explained to Albert Einstein (the great scientist I mentioned earlier) he is said to have retorted, "God does not play at dice!"

As I said to you before, some of our scientists resort to the word "God" because, even though they are not theists, many of them are searching for what they call a "Theory of Everything"—one principle that will explain everything else. The concept of God has remained convincing largely because it has for so long played this very role by delivering people from the uncomfortable suspicion that they were mere playthings of chance.

But it is this same understanding of God that is threatened by the rediscovery of the role of chance in the natural processes. I say "rediscovery" for at least you and Democritus can be cited as those who drew attention to it in ancient times, and we can now confirm its truth. However unique and important we may regard ourselves to be, each of us exists as the result of an almost infinite succession of chance events. And because chance played such an important role in the biological evolution that produced the human race—in addition to who we are as individuals—we can say that God (or Nature) does play at dice after all!

But of course I knew nothing of what you've just told me when I said that **all alike are subject to time and chance.**

Quite true; and that fact makes our rediscovery of your words all the more interesting. Your acknowledgement of the role of chance may also help to explain why you took no interest in the historical events that form the theme of the Torah, the events which your Jewish compatriots loved to call "the mighty acts of God." As you know, they believed that when Moses delivered your ancestors from slavery in Egypt, eventually to take possession of the Land of Promise, it was to fulfil God's purpose for them. They came to think of God as the one who controlled history, blessing them with victories over their enemies and punishing them for their sins when they suffered defeat.

We all tend to look for some sort of underlying purpose in history. It seems to be an inherent part of human nature to search for a reason for everything that happens to us and around us. This is because we feel much more confident living in an ordered and purposeful world, and tend to feel unsettled by the recognition of chance events. Even lovers like to think they were meant for each other from the beginning of time.

Yes, I suppose that theme, like the desire to find order in the world, must be nearly as old as humanity. But in the end I quite agree with you, for I find no evidence in the world of any underlying purpose in the events of history. **An evil that I have observed in this world, one that weighs heavily on people, is this: God may give a person such wealth, possessions and honour that he could wish for nothing more, and yet take from him the power to enjoy them and allow a stranger to possess them instead. This makes no sense; it's a dreadful wrong.**

Of course it is, if you think of God as the controller of history. That's why Job complained that the way the events of history unfold makes God seem morally unjust. Let me remind you that in your day you were already using the word *elohim* as a synonym for Nature. If *elohim* is regarded as a personal God then he could be accused of being immoral. But just as Nature is amoral and has no special interest in us, so the events of human history occur more by chance than as the result of any underlying purpose.

Thus when you speak of God you sometimes mean what the ancients called "the gods," you sometimes mean what Jew, Christian and Muslim called God, you sometimes mean what we call Nature, and you sometimes mean what is often called Luck. When it is to our advantage we call it Good Luck, and when it is to our hurt we call it Bad Luck. Moreover it is quite common for people to personify luck, as you still personify God; they speak of Lady Luck. Let's hear again what you wrote if we translate *elohim* as luck:

Luck may give a person such wealth, possessions and honour that he could wish for nothing more, and yet take from him

the power to enjoy them and allow a stranger to possess them
instead. This makes no sense.

It is interesting you say "this makes no sense," for there is no purpose to be discovered in either luck or chance. Only yesterday I was reading a novel by a man called John Mortimer, who created a fascinating character he named Rumpole. Listen to what I found Rumpole saying: "I have come to the conclusion that life is a game of chance like roulette, and not a game of skill like chess. There seems to be no sense or logic in the cards we are dealt."

And why does life often appear to make no sense? It's because luck—that is, pure chance—is completely lacking in purpose. So your words strike us as thoroughly modern precisely because today we are much more ready to acknowledge the role of chance in the world. The word "Luck" is as much on everybody's lips today as the word "God" used to be in the past. Where people used to say "God be with you" when they parted, now they are likely to say "Good luck on your journey." We know there is no certainty about the future (as you yourself often said) and this is because it is to a large degree dependent on chance events.

It's because chance so often determines the events in life that
I gave up looking for any purpose. **Let me tell you what I've**
come to realise: It's good and proper simply to eat and drink,
and take satisfaction in all the work we do on the face of the
earth. After all, this is our human lot during the limited days
of life that Nature gives us.

Does that mean that you advise us to fasten our attention primarily on the present rather than worry about the future? Strangely enough Jesus said something very like that—"Do not be anxious about tomorrow but let tomorrow be anxious about itself. The troubles each day brings are enough for that day."

I agree with that man Jesus. Why worry about the future?
Indeed, no one knows the future, for who can tell what is to

come? To worry about the future is the same as worrying about when we will die. After all, no person knows when his appointed time will come. No man has control over the breath that gives life, so no one can decide the day of his death.

In short, you're advising us to accept what each day brings, being neither over-optimistic nor over-pessimistic, but ready for the surprises that may come in a world where luck often seems to play a vital role. In other words, our lives are not being ordered by some unseen power for some ultimate purpose unknown to us. Life comes with one guarantee only, and that is death.

Exactly so! For to everyone whom Luck has blessed with wealth and luxuries, it has also given the power to enjoy them, to accept his lot and find enjoyment in his work. This is a gift from Nature. But seldom will a person ponder the meaning of his life when Luck fully occupies him with gladness of heart.

So you think that those who enjoy good luck can go through life without being prompted to look for any meaning. But what about those who have not been blessed with good luck? Why does Nature seem to have something quite different in store for them?

This, then, is another dreadful evil—that just as a man comes, so he must go. What does he gain for himself by having toiled in pursuit of the wind? He has spent all his days in darkness and mourning, suffering great anger, sickness and wrath.

It seems to me we just have to accept that the life Nature doles out to us is shaped more by luck than by any underlying ultimate purpose. But if we have to accept whatever comes our way, whether good or bad, would it not be wise for us to try to take control of our own destiny where we can and create a future we would enjoy?

Create your future? Let me warn you! **All of a man's efforts are to fill his belly, yet his appetite is never satisfied. So what advantage has a wise man over a fool? What advantage does a poor man gain by knowing how to deal with life's problems? It's better to be satisfied with what's in front of you than to long for distant pleasures—for that, too, is as futile as chasing after the wind.**

In suggesting future planning I was not thinking of longing for distant pleasures. Like you, Jesus also warned us against such a plan—"Do not lay up for yourselves treasures on earth, where moth and rust consume and thieves break through and steal." I was thinking more of the wisdom of living a prudent life. Is that not something to be commended?

The prudent life consists of taking things as they come and enjoying them as much as you can.

So, if I may coin a phrase from your comments about time, you believe feasting and enjoying life have their place.

Indeed I do! Did I not say there is **a time to laugh and a time to dance about? So go and eat your food with gladness, and drink your wine with a joyful heart, for Nature has already given approval for you to do this.**

But when are the right times?

You must be the judge of those yourself. If you're on the lookout for them, you will recognize them when they come. **But take care! Be well dressed for every occasion, and be presentable in every way.**

Ecclesiastes, at last you sound encouraging. Surely you must have realised that many readers of your book find your words quite depressing; yet here you are telling me you really believe that life can be enjoyable.

I do indeed! So I say, **Enjoy life with a wife you love through all the days of the fleeting life that Nature has given you in**

this world. And know that this is your reward in life for the
toil and drudgery you have performed in this world.

That seems to me to be a positive and indeed admirable philosophy of life. Incidentally, it appears to comport rather well
with Jesus' attitude—even though it caused him to be labelled
a drunkard and a friend of scoundrels. So why are you not
content simply to pursue this philosophy without worrying any
further about whether life has meaning or purpose? Why do
you keep trying to find something else in life to deplore?

Well this is how I see it. A man may father a hundred children
and live many years; yet however many be the days of his
life and however elaborate his funeral, if he cannot enjoy his
prosperity, then, I say, a stillborn child is better off than he.
Though it arrives in futility and departs in darkness and its
name is shrouded in gloom, though it never saw the sun and
knew nothing, yet it has more rest than does the man, who
lives a thousand years twice over but gains no benefit from
his prosperity. Do not all go to the same place?

True! The good things we enjoy in life do not last forever and
death overcomes us all in the end. Yet some of the things we
either do or say actually survive us by the way they affect other
people. Isn't it time we started talking about our dependence
upon one another and what we should do to nurture the social
side of human existence? Most of our discussion so far seems
to assume that we have to face the challenges of life as lone
individuals.

I think I understand what you're getting at. Indeed I know
that it is said, "Two are better than one, because they receive
a good return for their work."

Yes, and that maxim is highly regarded in the business world
to this day, and is the reason smaller companies often find
themselves being swallowed by large corporations. But I was not
thinking of anything so commercial. Tell me, don't you think

we can and should assist one another when we suffer misfortunes that unfairly afflict us?

Of course, we need to assist one another when we are threatened by enemies. **Though assailants may overpower one person, two will be able to withstand them. A cord of three strands is not easily broken.**

And that insight is often followed today at an international level. Nations enter into non-aggression pacts or treaties to counter the kind of large-scale aggressive behaviour that has been all too prevalent throughout history. Because of two world wars in the twentieth century, we have now set up a vast organisation called the United Nations. But is it not just as important to give one another mutual support on a more personal level?

It is **true enough that if the one fails, the other can help him, but woe to the one who falls without someone to help him up!**

That's what I'm getting at. We humans have become what we are today only because of the strong personal relationships that bind us together in families, tribes and societies. Surely it is by mutual support of one another that we can best deal with the pain of the many burdensome aspects of human existence that you make so much of.

Again, I agree with you for **if two lie down together, they will keep warm, but how can a person keep warm if alone?**

That simple way of putting things reminds me very much of some words of Richard Rubenstein in his book *After Auschwitz*. He is not only a Jew like yourself, but a rabbi. Here is his description of the role of Judaism in the modern secularized world: "It is the way we Jews share our lives in an unfeeling and silent cosmos. It is the flickering candle we have lighted in the dark to enlighten and warm us."

I have never heard a Jew in my day say such a thing.

But neither did many Jews in your day speak as you did. Indeed, even though you are separated by more than two thousand years of rabbinical Judaism, you and Rubenstein appear to have much in common. You both concluded that life in this world is not controlled by any supernatural power or created for any ultimate purpose. And in both cases, what led to that conclusion were the gross injustices you observed in the world.

So what injustice led Rabbi Rubenstein to say it?

It was the fact of the Holocaust. I have mentioned this to you before. Because the German Nazis deliberately killed some six million Jews in their gas ovens and no divine hand was there to save them, Rubenstein argued that it was no longer possible to believe that there is a God who acts meaningfully in history. For him God has become the "Holy nothingness that offers only dissolution and death as the way out of the dilemmas of earthly existence."

*Have I not consistently deplored the meaningless disasters that occur in this world? It is because of them that **I came to hate life, because whatever happens in this world causes me distress. Everything is as futile as chasing after the wind.***

But consider that because of the Holocaust, Rubenstein had even more reason than you to be distressed by what goes on in the world, and yet I doubt if he would agree with you that everything we do is as futile as chasing after the wind. He still finds a use for the Jewish tradition; its practices provide some light and warmth in this cold and unfeeling cosmos. You seemed to hint at something similar when you said that "if two lie down together, they will keep warm."

That's really the key to the origin of the synagogue. During your lifetime this institution was still in its embryonic stage, and this may explain why you don't refer to it or show any interest in it. When you ancient Jews lost everything you depended upon—your own land, the monarchy, the temple—you began to come together to support one another in your tragic loss. The word synagogue simply means "coming together."

It was an entirely new religious institution, and having neither priest nor altar, it has been described as a layman's institute for study and discussion. It was the prototype for the later rabbinical synagogue, the Christian church and the Muslim mosque. These were very simple at first, though over the centuries they took on their traditionally religious or supernatural trappings. But now that we have entered a more secular world, that early synagogue may be a clue as to how we can support one another in a world that operates more by chance than for any ultimate purpose.

Indeed Robert Bellah, a sociologist of religion, has said that in today's world each individual must formulate his or her own ultimate answers to the quest for meaning, and that the most a synagogue, church, or mosque can do "is to provide a favourable environment for doing so without imposing a prefabricated set of answers."

There are no absolute and final answers to the quest for meaning in life, for the element of chance can rob life of much of its meaningfulness, as you've correctly argued. But we humans apparently have within us the potential to make life meaningful. Perhaps that's what the quest for wisdom has always been. Let's take that for our subject next time.

9

WHY SEARCH
FOR WISDOM?

I would like to find out from you, Ecclesiastes, what prompted you to set out in search for wisdom. What did you expect to find? You appear to have ignored the teaching of the priests and the oracles of your Jewish prophets. These two professional classes, each in their own way, believed that the truth they proclaimed had come from a divine source rather than being something they had arrived at by their own efforts. You, on the other hand, seem to have rejected divine revelation as a source of useful knowledge. Is that because you believe the wisdom you seek in your observations of the real world will prove more reliable than their pronouncements?

I do indeed! **It is said, "Wisdom makes the wise man more powerful than the rulers of the ten cities."**

If that were true, it would certainly provide a powerful incentive for the pursuit of wisdom. But must we not distinguish between wisdom and knowledge? In our world today there has been a veritable explosion of knowledge and it's this, rather than wisdom, that can make us powerful. Further, I doubt whether we can claim a similar increase in wisdom. In fact I sometimes wonder whether very ancient people who lived close to nature and to the land were not actually wiser than we.

Do not say, "How is it the olden days were better than these?" For this question does not arise from wisdom. *Indeed, the great accumulation of knowledge you have described to me practically guarantees that people of your day must understand* *the world better than we ancients, and therefore must be considered wiser.*

Very well! I shall refrain from trying to compare the wisdom of one age with that of another. But I would like to find out what prompted you to get started on your search for wisdom.

Since the time I was young, **I have heard it said, "Wisdom is more profitable than folly, just as light is more valuable than darkness. The wise man has his eyes in his head, but the fool walks in darkness.** *" So that set me off on my search. Now, I would go even further in condemning folly, and say that* **a fool's efforts so weary him that he doesn't even know his way back to town.**

I like your sense of humour, but you speak of wisdom as if being wise is just a matter of developing sound common sense and of avoiding making a fool of oneself. Admittedly, much can be said in favour of being guided by common sense. We all have a modicum of it, though some seem to be more endowed with it than others. In every culture that kind of wisdom becomes encoded in little sayings we call proverbs, such as "A stitch in time saves nine."

Of course that's the way the pursuit of wisdom starts, as many of the proverbs in the Jewish book of that name make quite clear. Indeed I began to collect a few of these gems myself. Here is one of them: **Let your words be few, for just as dreaming results from an abundance of tasks, so the voice of a fool manifests itself in the abundance of his words.**

That's a timely warning to those whose words are so rapid and thoughts so sluggish that they rattle on with little or no thought to what they are saying. But I am more particularly struck by your comment about dreaming. Even up until recent times many people took dreams to be messages from another world, or perhaps prophecies of things to come. Not until the 20th century did our psychologists make a scientific study of this common experience and begin to find by their analysis how dreams, far from bringing messages from an external world, actually often convey useful information about what is going on inside our minds. So I'm very impressed to learn that even in your day you were aware of a correlation between dreams and the mental tensions we experience in daily life.

Oh yes, we know about dreaming and sleeping. Indeed it is common for us to say: **Sweet is the sleep of the worker whether he eats little or much, but the feast eaten by the rich man causes him to toss and turn.**

Ah yes, another of your gems! So you started your pursuit of wisdom by simply making a collection of the wise sayings or proverbs that you found in your culture.

Of course! Another one I rather like is this: **As fast as one's goods increase, so does the number who gather to consume them.**

That reminds me of what we call Murphy's law, which states that if something can go wrong, it will.

Aha, so some of your contemporaries agree with me! That's why I followed the previous observation with this one: **What advantage are they to their owner except for him to feast his eyes on them?** *And that's why I keep saying:* **This shows the futility of seeking wealth.**

I now realise from what you say that you did not actually compose everything in your book. In this way you've helped me understand that Jewish wisdom was an ongoing oral tradition: successive generations of sages drew from it and also added their own personal contributions. This tradition must have gone back to time immemorial—at least to the time of Solomon. And, as I can now tell you, it continued after you through such sages as Jesus ben Sirach, the author of *The Wisdom of Solomon* and down as far as Jesus of Nazareth.

Just as you confess you were sometimes simply quoting common sayings from this ongoing tradition, so from time to time

Jesus also quoted his predecessors. For example, many people today incorrectly believe that Jesus was the first to say "Love your neighbour as yourself," but he was simply reciting what he found in the Torah. However, when Jesus said, "Love your enemies and pray for those who persecute you" he was surely breaking new ground.

That's certainly a striking injunction. But do you not realise that its general thrust was already present in the Wisdom tradition? Have you not read in the Book of Proverbs, "If your enemy is hungry, give him bread to eat, and if he is thirsty, give him water to drink"?

I find it interesting that you are re-directing my attention to the ideas behind the words rather than to the authority of the person who proclaimed them. In our cultural tradition the reverse seems to have been all too common. People have always liked to appeal to authority, and they still often say, "The Bible says . . . ," as if that clinches the matter. Of course, in the Bible itself the words of Jesus were considered paramount by Christians.

What difference does it make who actually first enunciates a maxim or composes a wise saying? With true gems of wisdom it is not who *said it but* what *is said that really matters.*

That may be true, yet we often take more notice of an injunction if it comes with the authority of someone we highly respect. Did not you, the Proclaimer, deliberately put your words into the mouth of Solomon, the wise man par excellence, in the expectation that your readers would consequently take them more seriously?

You've misunderstood my intention. That was simply a literary convention that has been common in Jewish culture. We see the pursuit of wisdom as a joint venture by unnamed sages and not the prerogative of a few special individuals. That's why I've refrained from telling you anything about myself. It's

not I you should be concerned about, but my words. I am sim-
ply the anonymous Proclaimer. You should think deeply about
what is being proclaimed and test out these insights and max-
ims for yourself.

You seem to be undermining the idea of authority that has
been deeply embedded in our monotheistic cultures. Perhaps
this is why, though a Jew yourself, you never refer to the Torah.
In the rabbinical tradition Jews have regarded the Torah as absolute because it was delivered to Moses by God. For Christians
that divine authority was extended to the whole Bible. Similarly,
Muslims believe the Qur'an came to Muhammad from Allah.
As I said, even the words of the sage Jesus carry a great deal
more weight just because it was he who said them.

Let me ask you a question about this Jesus whom you claim
to be a sage. Is it the case that people paid attention to what
he said because he was already held in honour, or was it the
striking nature of his words that caused people to come to
honour him?

An excellent and perceptive question! When you put it that
way, I have to agree it was the latter. Even the Gospels tell how
this previously unknown Galilean began to draw large crowds
to hear him because they found his words and parables so ar-
resting. It was the quality of his teaching that led to his growing
reputation, and only after his fame spread did people come to
regard him as the Messiah and make all sorts of fantastic claims
about him.

Since I am offering you occasional examples of Jesus' unique,
contributions to the Wisdom tradition, let me ask you how you
went about the task of adding to the accumulation of wisdom?

*It was by **taking note of all the happenings that occur on***
***earth.** These, for example, are some of the simple things that I*
*observed. **He who digs a pit may fall into it. He who breaks***
through a wall may be bitten by a snake. The quarryman
may be injured by a stone or a wood-splitter by a log.

So wisdom alerts a person to the various accidents that may possibly occur in daily life, thus prompting him to take the necessary precautions against hidden dangers.

Exactly so! **If the wedge is blunt or the axe unsharpened, he will have to apply excessive force, but wise foresight will help him to succeed. If a serpent bites before it is charmed, there is no value in the charmer's art.**

I can see that for you wisdom consists, in part, of learning the skills necessary for using tools. It's therefore something naturally sought by all artisans and artists. But surely wisdom is also much more than that! The American philosopher Henry Thoreau defined a philosopher as one who solves the problems of daily living more expertly than do his neighbours.

I thoroughly agree with him. Wisdom has to do with the art of living and finding our proper place in society. **Words from a wise man's mouth win favour, but the lips of a fool lead to his undoing. When he first opens his mouth, his words make no sense and by the end of his speech they become incriminating madness, but still the fool babbles on and on.**

We have people like that too! At first their volubility gives us the impression of wisdom, but we eventually wake up to the fact that they are merely babbling. Still, surely little harm is done, for we can simply ignore what they say. Or do you think that foolish talk can be harmful?

I certainly do. Wisdom leads to fruitful actions; but foolish talk, if listened to, can lead us all into all sorts of disasters. **It takes only one evil-doer to lay waste a mountain of good.** *Remember what I said:* **As dead flies make the perfumer's ointment stink, so a little folly can overpower much wisdom and honour.**

You have a vivid way of describing the consequences of folly, but so far you've been rather vague about the nature of wisdom. If folly can do such harm, what sort of advantages can result from wisdom?

Wisdom gives us insight and motivates us. **The heart of the wise person inclines him to the right, but the heart of the fool to the left. Lacking sense, a fool has only to walk along the road to show everyone what a fool he is.**

There you go again, simply contrasting a wise person and a fool. It still does not tell me what you regard as the essence of the wisdom you seek. Can you be more precise on what you think the acquirement of wisdom will actually do for people?

The possession of wisdom enables them to understand the world around them and to find the best way to live with others so as to promote the common good. **A wise mind knows the proper time and procedure. There is a proper time and procedure for every enterprise, because of the widespread evil that people do.**

Aha, then wisdom is more than just common sense; it brings a special kind of insight. When you said you decided to set out in search of wisdom, you implied that it is something to be acquired. Right at the beginning of our discussion you likened wisdom to light. That makes me wonder if you expect the pursuit of wisdom to lead to some form of enlightenment.

To some degree that could be true. **A person's wisdom lights up his face and the grimness of his appearance is transformed.**

Now that description would fit the experience of Gautama the Buddha. You may recall something I said in an earlier conversation—that you and he shared the idea of the impermanence of everything. His followers have long venerated him by creating images of him. (I have two of them in my study, for I feel a certain attraction to him myself). And these images portray him as a very happy and contented person who, having reached an important goal in life, was keen to enable others to do the same.

And why was he called the Buddha?

Buddha is a title meaning "the enlightened one"—for that is why he came to be honoured. But his enlightenment came only after a great struggle. Though born into a royal household, he is said to have abandoned wealth and comfort in order to go in search of spiritual truth. It makes me wonder whether you would have described this as the pursuit of wisdom. One after another he tried out the traditional paths to spiritual wisdom, looking for the solutions to the basic questions that worried him; but he found none of them satisfying. In a state of despair he sat down under a bo-tree and determined not to shift until he found what he was seeking. On that very spot he at long last experienced what he called enlightenment.

However, this was not the kind of knowledge that can be recorded and passed on in language. It was evidently an inner experience of complete contentment. The problem that chiefly concerned him—how to be delivered from everlasting suffering—was apparently solved. On achieving this enlightenment, the Buddha travelled throughout India, the country of his birth, joyfully inviting others to share his experience by following the eight-fold path that he prescribed.

Is that why you immediately thought of this man when I said, **A person's wisdom lights up his face and the grimness of his appearance is transformed?**

It is indeed! You strike me as a person who may be compared with the Buddha, for you both set out on a search for wisdom. You even suggest that wisdom, when experienced, is rather like "seeing the light." But when I read where your search eventually led you, I find your experience was quite different from that of the Buddha. Although I'm sure his followers would regard him as a very wise man, his wisdom was evidently not the kind that you were looking for. So how would *you* describe the wise man?

He is not easy to describe for **who can be compared with the wise man? Who else knows the meaning of things?**

Aha, then in your view the wise man is one "who knows the meaning of things." We call such a man a philosopher. When we examine the roots of the word "philosophy," we find it comes from two Greek words meaning "the love of wisdom." And indeed, wisdom and philosophy have much in common. Perhaps that's why, in your language, the pursuit of wisdom was the only way of referring to what we now call philosophy. As a matter of fact, when Hebrew was recently revived as a living language in modern Israel it had to borrow the Greek word "philosophy," just as we did.

So does your stated determination to seek wisdom mean you decided to become a philosopher? If so, that would help to explain why you so often question what others take for granted. We have long associated this critical kind of philosophy with the ancient Greeks, and our Western culture's dedication to empirical thinking owes a great deal to them. The greatest of the Greek philosophers— Socrates, Plato and Aristotle—lived only a century or two before you. But, as I said before, you don't appear to have known about them. That makes it all the more interesting that you were quite independently voicing questions not unlike some that the Greek philosophers had recently raised.

You must tell me more about these Greek philosophers, for perhaps I do have something in common with them.

There was one Greek philosopher, in fact, who seems to have been your contemporary in time. He was Zeno of Citium, who went from Cyprus (not all that far from where you lived), set up his own school at Athens at the Stoa, and became the originator of stoicism, a philosophy destined to have widespread influence in the West. It even had some impact on Christian thought, for Paul, the man who did most to spread Christianity, was brought up in the city of Tarsus, a great centre for Stoic philosophy.

Tell me more about this Zeno.

In some respects he was a man after your own heart. He said
we should learn to accept the disagreeable things that happen
in life just as we should gratefully accept the good things, for
they are all part of the way nature works. Indeed, his understanding of God was not unlike your own in that the word
symbolically referred to the way the natural world works. He
was also a humanist in that he was much more concerned with
our common human traits than with celebrating tribal and
ethnic identity. He favoured the emergence of a cosmopolitan
republic where all were equal—where not even the wise man
exerted any power over his fellows but was simply a citizen
dutifully doing what nature requires. In a similar way, Jew
though you are, you seem to have been more interested in the
universal human condition than in the history and destiny of
your own people.

First you liken me to the Buddha and now you say I have
much in common with Zeno. But these two men seem to have
been very different.

Indeed they were; but all three of you had something important in common: you all asked basic questions about human
existence. The difference is that you asked them in different
ways. One of the important distinctions between Gautama
the Buddha and Zeno the philosopher is that the Buddha
was searching inside himself for the answers to his questions,
whereas Zeno fixed his attention on the world around him.
How did *you* go about your search for wisdom?

I gave my full attention to the study of wisdom, taking note of
all the happenings that occur on earth.

That confirms just what I suspected; you are more like Zeno
than the Buddha. It could even be said (if I may use terms
we have learned from a modern psychologist, Carl Jung) that
whereas the Buddha was an introvert (seeking to look inside
himself), you and Zeno were extroverts, looking outside of
yourselves for the answers to your questions. Did you gain

some degree of personal satisfaction as you progressed in your search?

My soul rejoiced in all I had achieved, for this was my reward for all my effort.

Yet, as time went on you evidently became less than completely satisfied in your search for wisdom, for sometimes you sound downright pessimistic. And each time I encounter this shift in your mood it catches me somewhat off balance. Can you think of any incident that may have sparked off your change of attitude?

Yes! I also saw something else in this world—an example of wisdom that greatly impressed me. Once a small city, with only a few people in it, was attacked by a powerful king who surrounded it and built huge siegeworks against it. Now it happened that in that city lived a poor but wise man, and he could have saved the city by his wisdom. Yet nobody remembered that poor man!

Ah, I think I begin to understand you better now. This is another of your parables, one that's even closer in kind to those of the great sage Jesus of Nazareth. But there is something about this story of yours that suggests to me the possible memory of a historical incident. Among the Greek philosophers you wanted to know more about was one named Socrates, who is sometimes described as the "the wise man *par excellence.*"

He lived in Athens a century or two before your day, during a time when the neighbouring Spartans (who gloried in their military prowess) attacked Athens and besieged it. Socrates strongly advised against accepting the Spartan challenge to fight, and urged his fellow citizens to negotiate a peaceful settlement. His words were ignored, with the result that the city of Athens was sacked.

That does not surprise me. It simply exemplifies what I used to say: **As there is no avoidance of battle in time of war, so wickedness will not save those who are masters of it.**

But now listen to the tragic end of the story. When peace was restored and the city rebuilt, Socrates was arrested and charged with some trumped-up accusation of corrupting the youth of Athens. Sad to say, he was sentenced to death by drinking poison. And it seems to me worth noting that Socrates was later honoured by the Stoics, who saw his role as rather like that of Jesus for the Christians. In fact, your little parable of the wise man who was tragically ignored fits the story of Socrates so perfectly that I cannot help thinking some account of him must have reached you. In any case, I am sure you'd have admired him and would agree with the wise counsel he offered to his fellow Athenians. Isn't that so?

I do indeed! **I say, "Wisdom is better than strength" even though the poor man's wisdom was despised and his words went unheeded.**

Well, I'm glad we are in agreement on that. Still, although you clearly affirm what an asset it is to possess wisdom, I am still unclear as to what you assume wisdom to be. Here, for example, you seem to be equating wisdom not with knowledge derived from observation, but with sound, measured judgment of the kind we may arrive at in a crisis following a period of quiet and adequate reflection on all the issues involved.

Every crisis calls for a cool head. **Wisdom is better than weapons of war. The quiet words of the wise are more to be heeded than the ranting of a master of fools.**

I can see you'd be very derisive of the kind of rhetoric that politicians and preachers in our day often resort to in times of crisis. No doubt you'd urge them to display the kind of wisdom shown by the poor man in your story. But this brings us back to why you told me the story in the first place; it was in answer to my question of how you first began to have doubts about your pursuit of wisdom.

The reason is this: **after giving my full attention to the acquisition of wisdom—as well as to the understanding of** *madness and folly—I realised that this too is like chasing after the wind.*

How can you say that? Surely the acquisition of wisdom brings its own reward; indeed you seemed to say as much in your own initial experience.

But this "reward" you speak of does not last. Let me give you an example. Wouldn't you say that it's better to be a poor but wise youth than an old and foolish king who can no longer even take care of himself?

I certainly would. To me that seems almost self-evident.

And would you further agree that to be true, even if from the prison house the youth has gone forth to rule or perhaps was born poor in what was to become his own kingdom?

Of course! That would make it one of those "poverty to riches" tales that people delight in. Surely that would show how the possession of wisdom can finally triumph.

But for how long does the sense of triumph last? You see I have been observing those who are now living. They side with the youth who takes the king's place—and perhaps also would no end of people who lived before them both—but as for the generations yet to come, they will find no joy in him at all. So this too—this striving for eminence and acclaim—is as futile as chasing after the wind.

But why should you turn away from the pursuit of wisdom just because later generations may have no knowledge of what has gone before and hence show no interest in particular examples of the eminence and acclaim to which it may lead?

It made me realise that the possession of wisdom does not necessarily lead to any permanent happiness. Indeed, with the increase of wisdom comes the increase of grief; for the more we know, the greater our sorrow.

But if you were beginning to find the pursuit of wisdom just as futile as you found so much else in life, where else could you turn?

So I said to myself, "Very well! Let me try pleasure and enjoy myself."

My immediate reaction to that, if you'll pardon my saying so, is to question whether that was a wise decision on your part. But then, I suppose, if the pursuit of wisdom was not providing what you expected from it, the obvious thing was to focus your attention on pleasure itself. So how did you go about your pursuit of pleasure?

I denied myself nothing my eyes desired; I refused my heart no pleasure.

You seem to have adopted a way of life that some in every generation turn to when they become disillusioned with life. They surrender all self-discipline, ignore the social requirements of acceptable behaviour, spend their money recklessly, and indulge their bodily appetites. So I'm interested to learn if you found any more satisfaction by simply pursuing pleasure for its own sake.

What did I find? "It too is short-lived." As for laughter, I said "It is foolishness!" And with regard to pleasure, "What can this achieve?"

That does not surprise me in the least. The most satisfying pleasures we experience are those that come as by-products of other activities. For example, denying ourselves something in order to bring joy to somebody else can strangely enough bring pleasure to us. On the other hand, when pleasure is sought for its own sake, it often seems flat, unsatisfying and disappointing when it comes. So after finding your pursuit of pleasure a fruitless occupation, what did you do then?

As I felt compelled to try everything, I then racked my brain on whether to cheer my body with wine.

It must have been as a last resort that you thought of turning to wine, as so many people unfortunately also do to excess in our day. You may remember my telling you that our artist Colin McCahon, a man quite captivated by your words, sadly brought his own career to an end by doing just that. Surely that was a foolish idea for you even to contemplate.

*I did not choose it lightly and you must believe me when I say that **my mind was still guiding me into wisdom, and not yet captivating me with foolishness.***

I find that rather hard to believe. What made you imagine that it could have been a wise decision?

*All I said was that I racked my brain over the issue. After all, I had to investigate all alternatives and in the end I did not choose that one, **since my wisdom remained with me.***

And having turned away from wine, what did you do then?

So I turned my attention to the consideration of wisdom itself. I was determined to know the best course for people to take in this world, seeing the days of their lives are so limited. I said to myself, "I am resolved to become wise."

You sound again like the Buddha sitting under the bo-tree, determined to find the answer to his quest. And what did you find?

I saw that wisdom is but madness and folly.

That does not altogether make sense. How can wisdom be equated with folly when you've so often set out wisdom and folly as polar opposites?

What I meant was that the pursuit *of wisdom is folly. The reason is that **I found wisdom was beyond me.***

So you came to the conclusion that wisdom, of the sort you were seeking, is ultimately unattainable.

*That is exactly so! **Whatever wisdom may be, it is so distant and so deep that no one can discover it.***

Now you seem to be treating wisdom as if it were a kind of objective knowledge that is eternal, absolute and beyond all question. What was it that led you to the conclusion that it is impossible ever to reach this kind of wisdom?

When I gave my full attention to the study of wisdom, taking note of all the happenings that occur on earth, I saw that though a man sleep neither day nor night in his search to understand all the "works of God," he cannot find out what it is that God has done on the earth. However diligently a man may seek, he will not find out. Not even the sage who claims to know can find it out.

But this suggests to me that our discussion on wisdom has gone round in a circle. At the beginning I suggested we must distinguish between wisdom and knowledge but now you seem to be equating them. In our discussions we established that when you speak of "the works of God" you are referring to the way the natural world works. Today we simply call that scientific knowledge. It is not at all surprising that you found yourself frustrated in not being able to achieve such a goal, for even in our day—with all the knowledge we have gained, and with our sophisticated instruments of research—we are still far from reaching your impossible goal of knowing everything.

For even though we know much more than you ever imagined possible about the earth we live on, our new knowledge has opened up two whole new areas for research that you knew nothing of—the mega-world of far distant nebulae and star clusters, and the micro-world of the tiniest life forms and sub-atomic particles. You see, the more we know the more we find there is to know!

So when you saw you were seeking an impossible goal, what did you do then?

I shifted my attention to understanding, to exploring the nature of knowledge and reflection, so as to be aware of the stupidity of wickedness and the madness of folly.

In other words you turned back to what we call epistemology, the philosophy of knowledge. This branch of philosophy discusses what you yourself have called "the nature of knowledge" and how we arrive at knowledge we can feel confident about. Did you come to any satisfactory conclusion about this?

*Yes and no! Let me put it this way. I came to realise that **wisdom is best when combined with an inheritance and thus can benefit all on whom the sun shines. For the protection of wisdom may be like the protection of money, but it has the added advantage of knowing that wisdom preserves the life of those who possess it.***

Ah! When you say "wisdom is best combined with an inheritance," I detect a distinct element of cynicism. We have cynics today who dismiss theology and even philosophy as intellectual pursuits because in their view they get us nowhere. According to such people only money speaks and its power opens doors. If this were your intention in your remark, it would bring you a little closer to a group of Greek and Roman philosophers we call the "Cynics" and from whom we have derived the word "cynical."

Though we use that word today to refer to the rather sneering attitude of those who question human sincerity, the ancient philosophers were given the name "Cynics" for a more worthy reason. They were judged to show a dog-like attitude towards those intellectuals whose theories they regarded as useless. (In Greek, *kunikos* means canine). It is understandable that you should demonstrate a little of their attitude after you had become disillusioned with your pursuit of wisdom. The Cynics often made quite outrageous statements and did not care a fig what people thought of them because they thought it more important to jolt people out of their complacency.

*Although I've never heard of these Cynics, I also say: **do not pay attention to everything people say, or you may hear your servant disparage you. You know in your own heart how*** *many times you yourself have disparaged others. I have tested all this by wisdom.*

But even if you were somewhat cynical in your disillusionment, you still seemed to retain great respect for the sage or wise man. Is this because you began to see wisdom no longer as an objective body of infallible knowledge, but as a desirable human quality?

*Yes, you could put it that way. I still affirm that **it is better to heed a wise man's rebuke than to listen to the praise of fools. Like the noise of nettles crackling under kettles is the cackling of fools. But even the wise man's rebuke may be futile, for extortion can turn a wise man into a fool, and a bribe corrupt his mind.***

I am glad to hear you affirm that we should heed the wise rather than listen to fools. That suggests you think that your life-long struggle in the pursuit of wisdom, however unsuccessful, has nevertheless had its reward in making you a wiser, if even a sadder man?

*Up to a point that may be true. **And yet when I surveyed all that my hands had done, all that I had struggled to achieve, everything was as futile as chasing after the wind. I had made no gain at all in this world.***

Why is it that I am so unsuccessful in trying to persuade you to take a more positive view of life?

*It's because of how it all ends. Here I am near the end of my life, wondering what I've achieved. **So I said to myself, "Since the fate of the fool will be my fate also, then for what purpose have I become extremely wise?" Thus I concluded that even the pursuit of wisdom is futile. For in the long run the wise man is no more remembered than the fool, since everything will be forgotten as the future stretches on ahead. How on earth can it be that the wise man dies as does the fool?***

Why that is simply the way things are, as we have already discussed. I've tried to show you that the phenomenon of death
has a more positive role to play than you think. Besides, isn't it
better to die in the knowledge that you have lived well rather
than badly—perhaps even to have reason to believe you've left
the world a little better for having lived? Alas, it is only too
true that wisdom offers no escape from death, and that death
comes to the good and the evil alike. But what about our declining years, the time of old age that so often precedes death?
How should the sage navigate this portion of life's journey?
That should prove to be a most appropriate topic for our final
discussion.

10

CONCLUSIONS
ABOUT LIFE

Since this is to be our last encounter, Ecclesiastes, it's appropriate that we discuss some of your general conclusions about life before going on to the problems we humans all experience as we grow old. You described the latter very strikingly in the very last chapter of your book, yet you never revealed your age. Like some people today you may be reluctant to do so, but it's clear you speak out of a lifetime of experience and so you must have had plenty of time to ponder its problems.

Since the average life expectancy in your day was considerably lower than it is with us now, it's likely that you were no more than fifty or sixty years of age when you wrote down your reflections on life. Nevertheless, I somehow suspect you may have been a decade or so older. Since you felt you had lived long enough to have "seen everything" you must have some general observations concerning what you've found.

*Indeed I have! **The sum and substance of what I have found is that Nature endows people with the possibility of leading upright lives, but they have pursued many harmful devices.***

So you believe that, as infants, we are not only free from sin, but in fact have the potential to become virtuous people. In that case, it must be an unfortunate upbringing, unlucky experiences, or bad choices—and not some inherent predisposition to immorality—that causes us humans to fall into the evil ways that bring harm to others. And I take it you are referring to all of us, not only a minority?

Of course! But that doesn't mean that very many people live up to their high potential. **Look, this is what I have discovered as step by step I sought to reach a conclusion, and continued to search without finding it: I found one upright man in a thousand.**

That's not many, if, as you say, we all have the potential to become virtuous. But it is encouraging that you found some who were worthy of your praise, for that suggests the possibility may be there for all of us.

—and not one such woman among them all!

You can't be serious! That makes you sound like the kind of person we today call a male chauvinist. On second thoughts, perhaps it's unfair of me to expect your attitude toward women to be any different from that which prevailed in your day. After all, it's only in very recent times that women have been emancipated from the inferior place in society in which men long held them captive. Nevertheless, let me remind you of the Book of Proverbs, which I understand you have read. Its very last chapter (which incidentally in our Bible immediately precedes your own book) is almost wholly devoted to the womanly virtues of a good wife.

But even that chapter begins by asking, "Where is such a good wife to be found?" Surely that suggests that a good wife is difficult to find. And all I said was that in my search I had not found one upright woman.

Perhaps that's because in your times women were so hidden from the public eye that your empirical search was unduly restricted. Indeed the cultural practice of sequestering women in their homes meant that those who were most likely to be seen in public were the prostitutes. The Book of Proverbs warns men to be wary not only of prostitutes but of the loose woman who will try to seduce them while her husband has gone a long journey. I suspect that you may have shared this concern with the sages?

Yes I did and I still do! **I find more bitter than death the woman who is a snare. Her heart is a net and her hands are chains. The person innocent in the sight of God may escape her, but she will surely capture the sinner.**

I was afraid you may say something like that, for in our day we are slowly coming to accept gender equality. Yet even today, I sadly confess, women are often made to carry more blame than men for incidents of adultery and the practice of prostitution. How much more was that the case in your day! In this respect, Ecclesiastes, I'm sorry to say, however keen you were to draw attention to social injustice, you show yourself to be a man of your own time.

Well, since my experience gives me no evidence on which to base a judgment, I will not comment on your proposal that women should be treated as equal to men; nonetheless, I find the notion all but impossible to believe.

On that issue, it appears, we must simply agree to disagree, and so let's change the subject. What other warnings do you have?

Do not make light of the king even in your thoughts, nor disparage the rich even in the privacy of your bedroom, because a bird of the sky may carry away your words; some winged creature may report what you say.

I like the poetic touch with which you describe the spread of gossip; even today when we learn a secret we say, "A little bird told me." But on a more serious note, I'm interested and a little surprised to hear you say that it's wise to pay due respect to the rich and powerful, since they have it within their power to harm you or take away your freedom. I notice that it did not prevent you from sometimes accusing people in high places of lacking integrity and of treating unjustly those who were beneath them. So I assume this piece of advice refers more to those in authority who have also earned respect by what they have done.

I have always said, **happy are you, O land, when your king** **is of noble birth and your princes eat at a proper time, with** **self-control and are not drunkards.**

Well and good, but what should we do if we are ruled by a tyrant or a dictator?

Equally, I say **woe to you, O land, if you are ruled by an im-** **mature youngster and your princes feast in the morning.**

Yes, but you did not answer my question of what we should do in those circumstances. Should we not rebel against immature, dictatorial, or wicked rulers in the interests of justice for all? Let me tell you what we have done. During the last two or three hundred years we have increasingly replaced absolute monarchy with more democratic forms of government. But it has sometimes needed a social revolution for this to take place. Would you approve of such revolutions?

No, I would not! Revolution against the established order can *be a very dangerous procedure. In our times every city or society* *is always so open to attack from the outside that firm rule by* *a strong dynasty is a great asset, for it ensures security. That's* *why I always said:* **If the ruler's anger rises against you, do** **not leave your post. Steadiness and composure will redeem** **great offences.**

No doubt that's very good advice to the young and hot-headed. In order to establish their own identity, they are often too ready to be critical of those in authority. They may even join anarchist groups without thinking through the implications. Of course at your age in life you are well equipped to offer guidance to the younger generation. So what is your advice to people who are just reaching the responsibility of adulthood?

This is what I would say to them. Be happy, young man, **while you are young, and let your heart give you joy in the** **days of your youth.**

I'm glad to hear you say so, for so much of your book is dominated by the sense of futility of life that I thought you'd be more discouraging than that. I well remember my own final day at High School. It was the practice for all school leavers to file out through the front door (which normally only the staff were allowed to use); outside we were greeted by well-known Old Boys, the last of whom said to me, "You're out in the cold, cold world now!" Now you, to my surprise, are more encouraging than they, urging the young to enjoy themselves while they can.

I do indeed! I say to them: **Follow the impulses of your heart and the desires of your eyes, yet know that for everything you do God (or Nature as you've taught me to say) will hold you accountable.**

Accountable to Nature? But if Nature does not seem to have any special interest in us humans and may do us harm as readily as provide us with bounty, why do you say that we are accountable to it?

First of all we owe to it everything we value. As I have said again and again, **the best that anyone can do is to eat and drink and enjoy himself in his work. This too, I realised, is from the hand of Nature; for if it were not for it, who could eat or who could have any enjoyment?**

So you think it's because Nature appears to show motherly care for us, at least some of the time, that we owe her something in return?

Whether Nature cares for us or not, I cannot say. What I do know is that we are not free to do whatever we like. In all that we do, we must take account of the way the natural world works. We have to live responsibly, and within the parameters set by Nature, or else we shall suffer for it. As I have said to you before, we cannot alter Nature. Nature runs its course without respect to us; so we must accept its ways. **If the clouds are full of rain, they will empty it upon the earth. Whether a**

tree falls to the south or to the north, it must lie in the place
where it falls.

I find it very interesting that you insist that we take cognisance
of the ways of nature for, as I have mentioned before, in our
century we are becoming aware of previously unexpected ways
in which the forces of nature are threatening all life on this
planet. Only slowly are we humans coming to realise that we
have unthinkingly brought a coming nemesis on ourselves.

What is this nemesis you speak of?

It's this! Prophetic voices are warning us that worldwide disasters could occur within the present century. Through the current global warming, we face the possibility of rising sea levels,
more destructive storms, severe droughts, lack of pure air and
water, insufficient food, and pandemics. And these dire threats
result from our recent population explosion, our wasteful use
of the earth's resources, our growing pollution of the planet,
and our interference with the complex systems of Nature.

So your warning that Nature will hold us accountable is remarkably relevant; we are coming to learn how badly we have
failed in caring for the earth. We used to think we had dominion over the earth, and indeed it was the Jewish Torah that told
us so. Now we know that we face a grave global crisis, for as one
of our scientists, James Lovelock, has said, "We have been putting human rights before human obligations to the Earth and
all the other life forms we share it with."

I quite agree with that man. If we do not obey the ways of
Nature we shall suffer for it, whether the problems be massive,
as you say yours are, or relatively minor like some of my exam-
ples: extreme laziness results in the roof caving in, and leaky
homes are a sign of negligence.

Those examples simply reflect the way in which humankind
learned over the millennia to protect itself from the elements
and how, if it is not industrious and ever alert, it has only itself
to blame when inclement weather causes it to suffer. Jesus

made this very fact the basis of one of his parables about life. He said the man who is wise enough to build his house on firm foundations has nothing to fear when the storm comes, whereas the man who builds on shifting sands may have his home washed away completely.

It remains as true today as it was in your day that we cannot control the weather and must be prepared for all kinds of dangerous events. The dangers we humans are facing today, however, are massive because they are on such a global scale. Have you any suggestions as to how we should fulfil our obligations to Nature?

Yes I have. Remember what I said: **When you make a vow to Nature, do not dally in discharging it. Nature takes no delight in fools; therefore perform what you have sworn to do. It is better for you not to vow at all than make a promise and not keep it.**

You have pinpointed our human weakness straight away, though I'm sure you did not realise it. Indeed you've touched us where we are most vulnerable. Even those of us who have become aware of the crisis we face, and who agree that we must do something about it urgently, nevertheless fail to institute the necessary changes in lifestyle because we are so wedded to our affluent ways. We have world conferences during which most nations give at least lip service to dealing with the vital issues, but the net result is a great deal of talking followed by little or no appropriate action.

That's why I say, **Do not allow your mouth to lead your flesh into sin. And do not protest to the messenger, "My vow was a thoughtless mistake." Why cause Nature to be angry at what you say, and destroy the work of your hands? If you give free rein to futile dreams you will only be led to utter empty words. Remain firmly in awe of Nature.**

That's sound advice at any time, but particularly in our scientific and technological age. Because of our great success in discovering more and more about the natural world there has been a tendency for us to lose our sense of wonder as we uncover the marvels of nature. Fortunately we are now being forced to recover some of that sense of awe that was such a powerful feature of human experience in primitive times. To be sure, we have learned much about the evolution of life on this planet and marvel at its variety and complexity—yet, the question of how it all began still eludes us.

I'm not surprised. **Just as you do not understand how life begins, how it enters the embryo in the womb of a pregnant woman, so you cannot understand how Nature works to create everything that exists.**

Ah, but that's not wholly true. As it happens we do now understand a great deal of how nature works. The sum-total of our current knowledge would greatly surprise you. Not only is it impossible for me to pass this on to you in a few words, but no one individual can master more than a small fragment of the knowledge now available. For this we are dependent, as I have said before, on a large company of experts. This knowledge helps us to achieve the most extraordinary feats. Would you believe me if I tell you that we have sent men to the moon and back?

I certainly would not. That's quite impossible. The moon is up in the sky along with the stars. We humans are earth creatures. This is where we belong and this is where we must stay. As I said before, **God is in the sky and you are on the earth.** *So what you claim sounds like a lot of moonshine to me. Soon you will be telling me that you can control the weather.*

We may not be able to control the weather but we are able to forecast the weather conditions. You see we now have some quite complex gadgets for gathering all kinds of data, on the basis of which experts can tell us what sort of weather to expect for the next several days everywhere on earth.

*But even we attempt to forecast the coming of storms or droughts and have some limited success. You may be able to do better with the "data-gathering gadgets" you speak of but I'd be greatly surprised if you always get it right. For as I have consistently said, **Since no one knows what is yet to come, who can tell him what the future will bring?***

I must concede that we don't always get it right. Indeed we often make fun of our weather forecasters when they get it wrong.

*It has always been the same with us. That's why I have continually warned people not to wait indefinitely for the most favourable weather for planting, for it may not come. **He who keeps watching the wind will never plant, and he who stares at the clouds will never reap.** So it is more important simply to get on with life and do your best no matter what the weather conditions are. We must take whatever comes and then we shall find that **good food leads to laughter, wine makes life merry and money is the answer for everything.***

Do I detect another touch of your sly cynicism in that last comment? After all, you yourself did not find the accumulation of wealth to be any answer to *your* problems.

*No, I did not! Have I not already told you that **whoever loves money will never be satisfied by amassing it, nor the lover of riches with his income.** So you've clearly misunderstood what I said. Perhaps I shall make myself clearer if I put it this way: the hard work that leads to the making of money is the answer to everything. Even so, there is no guarantee that hard work will bring forth fruit.*

If there is no guarantee of success as a result of hard work, does it mean that we have to live by hope?

*Of course! Hope is an important element in life. As I have often said, **whoever remains in the company of the living has some hope.***

I'm glad to hear you say that, for the tone of much of your book gave me the impression that you had lost all hope in life. Perhaps you'd then agree with a well-known dictum of St. Paul that, along with faith and love, hope is one of the values that last forever.

Of course, as I see it, nothing lasts forever. Nevertheless while we still live hope plays an important role. This is because, as we agreed earlier, there is a great deal of chance in life. So I say, **Sow your seed in the morning, and at evening let not your hands be idle, for you do not know which undertaking will prosper, this one or that, or whether the two of them will do equally well.**

And do you see it the same for the man of business as for the farmer?

It is indeed! One has to work hard, show some initiative and then hope for the best. That's why I say, **Cast your bread upon the surface of the waters, because after many days you will get a return.** *But there is no guarantee of this. So be wise and* **divide it among seven ventures, or even eight, for you do not know what disaster may come upon the land.**

We commonly resort to that bit of worldly wisdom also: we say "Don't put all your eggs in one basket." I'm very glad to hear your words of encouragement to the young to work hard, to show some entrepreneurial skills, and to expect good things to happen. As I said before, you don't always sound so positive as that.

But I have consistently said **there is nothing better for a man to do than to eat and drink and enjoy himself in his work. Therefore banish anxiety from your heart and cast off the troubles of your body, for youth and its early vigour are short-lived.**

I imagine that in encouraging the youth to make the most of life while they are young and vigorous, you are remembering your own younger days. I get the impression that they were very happy times and that you look back to them with some degree of nostalgia.

*I do indeed! There are moments when I can recover that feeling when it seemed good to be alive, the sensation that **light is sweet; it's a joy for the eyes to see the sun.***

But evidently you lost that early innocence and unbounded hope because of your subsequent experiences in life. They made you take a more serious view of life, one that you came to express in a series of aphorisms, set out in verse couplets.

*Well, first I came to see that **a good name is better than precious ointment.***

Of course, that literal translation obscures your clever word play in Hebrew. We could try to preserve it by saying something like this—"It's better to possess lots of dash than pots of cash." We can all agree with that but thereafter, if you'll pardon my saying so, your couplets became increasingly doleful.

*I suppose you are referring to my observation—**Sorrow is better than laughter, because sadness of countenance matures the mind.***

Exactly so! Yet that reminds me of one of the sayings of Jesus, "Congratulations to those who grieve! They will be consoled." That was a promise of comfort to those who lived under oppression, but you seem to have a preference for sorrow over laughter. Why is that, when you've already encouraged the young to be happy and follow the impulses of their hearts?

*It's because we do not fully appreciate the happy times until we have experienced sorrow. That's why I said, **The mind of the wise empathises with the house of mourning, but the mind of the foolish revels in the house of pleasure.** Indeed I go further and say, **The day of death is better than the day of birth.***

That's altogether too extreme. You sound more and more like Job as he sat afflicted with loathsome sores from head to toe and bewailed his lot by exclaiming, "Why did I not die at birth, come forth from the womb and expire?" Certainly we can become very depressed under such conditions but deep depression prevents us from making a balanced judgment about the pros and cons of life.

*That may be so, but I still say that **it's better to go to a house of mourning than attend a house of feasting, inasmuch as death is the end of each of us—a fact that we who are living should take to heart!***

Ah, Ecclesiastes, you never allow our rejoicing in life to last for long! Just when everything is going well and we feel that life could not be better, you bring us back to face our mortality again.

*Exactly so! We must never let the joys of life blind us to its darker side. **So if a man lives for many years, let him rejoice in every one of them. But let him remember that the days of darkness will be many, and that everything hereafter is nothingness.***

Ah, yes, Nothingness! I fear I must agree with you there. Before I was born I was nothing, and at my future death I shall again enter nothingness. But I don't like being reminded of it.

*Why not? There is no point in living in a fool's paradise, a sort of make-believe world. In the long run you are much better to face the facts of life and live in the real world. And I say also to the young, **Therefore think of your grave in the days of your youth, before the days of trouble come and those years arrive when you say, "I no longer find any pleasure in life."***

Think of your grave in the days of your youth! You remind me of something I once read about Philip of Macedon, a man who lived not long before you. He appointed a slave to a rather unusual task; every morning he was to wake up the young king and say, "Master, remember you will some day die!" This is exactly what you are doing now when you warn the young to be aware all through their lives that some day they shall die. It reminds me that in an earlier discussion we agreed that Nature has made death an essential accompaniment of life.

Quite so! That's why my advice to the young is: **Think of your grave before the sun grows dim, and with it the daylight and the moon and the stars, and the clouds return after the rain.**

You are of course now referring to what happens to us when we grow old—the signs of deterioration of the physical frame and of the faculties that have served us so well during life. One by one we all grow old and tired and perhaps our faculties cease to function. Our sight begins to dim, just as you say. You remind me of the Seven Ages of Man, so wonderfully expressed by our much acclaimed bard, William Shakespeare. "The last scene of all," he said, "that ends this strange eventful history, is second childishness, and mere oblivion, sans teeth, sans eyes, sans taste, sans everything." What is more, you even display a touch of the bard's skill in the way you describe old age.

So let me continue in my kind of verse.
Think of your grave when the mind starts to wander
and the strong back begins to stoop,
when the disappearing molars cease to chew
and cataracts dim the eyesight.
Think of it when the doors to the street are closed
and the noise of the grinding mill fades,
when the sound of birds grows faint
and all the daughters of song are humbled.
Think of the grave when the fear of heights increases
and terrors lurk in the streets,
when the almond tree blossoms
and the grasshopper drags itself along
and desire is no longer stirred.
For humankind goes to its eternal home
and mourners go about the streets.
Think of the grave before the cord of life is severed,
the golden bowl is crushed,

the jar is shattered at the spring,
and the wheel is broken at the well.
For then the dust returns to the ground it came from,
and the spirit returns to the God who gave it.

No wonder we always find the approach of death such a humbling and solemn experience, one that so often has the effect of bringing us together to acknowledge our common humanity and the mortality we all share.

"Fast-fleeting," says the Proclaimer. "Impermanent!"
"Everything dissolves into nothingness"

So your last words, Ecclesiastes, are the same as your first. They have been your constant theme song. You felt the burden of impermanence so acutely that you concluded all effort was futile and there was nothing more to be said.

But what about the words in your book that follow that pronouncement? I have always assumed the conclusion reached by our scholars to be true; they are an epilogue added by an editor who, though fascinated by what you wrote, was also troubled by your conclusions. He thought readers should have the opportunity to be stimulated by your scepticism, but he did not want them to be led astray from God's eternal truth. So to guide and warn readers he made some comments on how he thought your book should be understood. In other words an editor, as it were, put you in your place.

But I'm having second thoughts on this score. I wonder if they might come from the very person I tried to discover in our first dialogue—the person who remains hidden behind the persona of Solomon. You'll recall, I trust, my observation that most of what you said reflected you own time and place rather than that of Solomon. Perhaps we are at last permitted to catch a tiny glimpse of the real you—or (should I say) hear a whisper of your own voice—as now, for a moment, you look back objectively at what you have written under the role of the Proclaimer. Just as a modern author, Robert Louis Stevenson, wrote his own epitaph before he died in Samoa, so you could well have written the epilogue to the words of the Proclaimer. Let me hear what you said.

The Proclaimer was not only wise in himself, but what is more important, he imparted his knowledge to the people. He searched and weighed and set forth a host of parables. The Proclaimer sought to find just the right words, and honestly write down what he found to be true.

It seems, then, that though the Proclaimer despaired of ever attaining any lasting wisdom because he found it always eluded him, you yourself believed it well worthwhile to record his thoughts. Why did you think that?

The words of the wise are like goads. They are like nails driven firmly home by members of a fraternity and now delivered by one caring guide.

At last you give me a clearer understanding of the role of the sage. It was not so much to attain eternal wisdom and pass it on, as it was to encourage others to join the search for wisdom by prompting them to think through issues for themselves instead of relying on the opinions and advice of others. That applies to the parables told by the sage Jesus also. Many of them end with an unexpected twist that was meant to jolt his listeners out of their stereotyped mindsets and work out their own solutions to the problems of life.

I now suspect that even in our discussions you were goading me somewhat. Certainly I did not always agree with the Proclaimer, and even where I did, I know that ours could not be the last word on the subject. Nevertheless, I'm very grateful for your words and have learned a great deal from them and from discussing them with you.

Apart from these, my son, be warned that there is no end to the making of books, and much study simply tires us out.

Your final warning about the multiplication of books reminds me of what one of the Gospel writers said about the sage

Jesus—"the world itself could not contain all the books that would be needed to record all that he said and did." In our day when libraries are filled to overflowing and a mass of information is available from the Internet at the click of a key on our computers, it is salutary to be reminded that however useful books may be, they are never able to provide all the wisdom we need for life.

I'm sad that this brings our encounter to an end. It has been so rewarding that I am reluctant to let you go, but I suppose I must.

That is the end of the matter, for now you've heard everything.

But have you not one final word?

Stand in awe of Nature and do what it requires of you, for this is the whole duty of humankind. For Nature will bring to judgment everything we do—even everything hidden, whether it be good or evil.

And nothing could be more appropriate than that for us humans in the modern world as we now grapple with immense problems, and largely of our own making. We must now leave you, Ecclesiastes, in your own place and time. That's where you will always belong, just as we belong to the twenty-first century. Yet precisely because you and I are both humans grappling with the basic problems of human existence, the twenty-three centuries that separate us have not prevented us from finding much common ground.

PART THREE

The words, and an afterword

11

THE BOOK OF
ECCLESIASTES

The thoughts of the Proclaimer, presented in the order in which
he bequeathed them and translated from the Hebrew language
and Jewish culture of the 3rd century BCE into the English
language and secular culture of the twenty-first century CE.

The Words of the Proclaimer, son of David, king in Jerusalem.
"Fast-fleeting," says the Proclaimer. "Impermanent!
Everything dissolves into nothingness."
What do we humans have to show for our life's work,
for all our efforts in this world, for all our sweat and toil?
One generation passes away and another takes its place.
It's only the earth that goes on for ever.

The sun rises and the sun sets,
and then it wearily returns to its place to rise once more.
The wind blows to the south, and then turns to the north;
it goes round and round and turns full circle.
All the rivers flow into the sea,
yet the sea never overflows.
Back to the place from which they arose,
the rivers return to flow once more.

All things become wearisome:
there's more to be said than a man can utter,
more to be seen than the eye can see,
more to be heard than the ear can hear.
Whatever has once existed will exist again

and past events will occur again,
for there is nothing new on the face of the earth.

Take anything of which people say,
"Look at that! It's new!"
Well, it already existed ages ago,
but long before our time.
There is no longer any memory of the ancient times,
just as future events will be forgotten by those who come later.

I, the Proclaimer, used to be the king over Israel in Jerusalem.
So I devoted myself to research,
to the rational understanding of everything
that happens on the face of the earth.
Ah, what an evil burden Nature has given
to the human race to busy itself with!

I studied all human activities,
everything that happens to people on the face of the earth.
And what have I found?
They are all as futile as chasing after the wind,
like a crookedness that cannot be made straight,
or a void that cannot be filled.

I said to myself, "Look! I've greatly increased in wisdom;
I've surpassed all who lived in Jerusalem before me.
My mind has absorbed a vast amount of knowledge and
    wisdom."
But after giving my full attention to the acquisition of
    wisdom—
as well as to the understanding of madness and folly—
I realised that this too is like chasing after the wind.
With the increase of wisdom comes the increase of grief;
for the more we know, the greater our sorrow.
So I said to myself, "Very well!

Let me try pleasure and enjoy myself."
What did I find? It too is short-lived.
As for laughter, I said "It is foolishness!"
And with regard to pleasure, "What can this achieve?"
Then I racked my brain on whether to cheer my body with
    wine
(my mind was still guiding me into wisdom,
and not yet captivating me with foolishness),
for I was determined to know
the best course for people to take in this world,
seeing the days of their lives are so limited.

I did things on a grand scale.
I built myself mansions and I planted myself vineyards.
I laid out for myself gardens and parks
and planted in them every kind of fruit tree.
I made myself reservoirs of water
to irrigate the orchard then sprouting with trees.
I acquired for myself slaves and servant-girls
even though I already had a large household
and already possessed cattle, sheep and goats
more numerous than all my Jerusalem forbears had owned.
I amassed for myself such treasures of silver and gold
as only kings and nations can boast.
I acquired men and women singers,
and what delights all men most—mistresses galore!
And so I grew great, surpassing all who had lived before me in
    Jerusalem.
I denied myself nothing my eyes desired;
I refused my heart no pleasure.
My soul rejoiced in all I had achieved,
for this was my reward for all my effort.
And yet, (since my wisdom remained with me)
when I surveyed all that my hands had done,
all that I had struggled to achieve,

everything was as futile as chasing after the wind.
I had made no gain at all in this world.

So I turned my attention to the consideration of wisdom itself,
and saw that wisdom is but madness and folly.
I have heard it said, "Wisdom is more profitable than folly,
just as light is more valuable than darkness.
The wise man has his eyes in his head,
but the fool walks in darkness."
But I myself have come to know
that the same fate overtakes them both.
So I said to myself,
"Since the fate of the fool will be my fate also,
then for what purpose have I become extremely wise?"
Thus I concluded that even the pursuit of wisdom is futile.
For in the long run the wise man
is no more remembered than the fool,
since everything will be forgotten as the future stretches
    on ahead.
How on earth can it be that the wise man dies as does the
    fool?

So I came to hate life,
because whatever happens in this world causes me distress.
Everything is as futile as chasing after the wind.
I hated all the wealth for which I had toiled under the sun,
wealth I must leave to the man who succeeds me—
for who knows whether he will be prudent or a fool?
Yet it is he who will control the fruits of my labour
and everything in which I have shown some skill in this world.
This is simply meaningless.

So I turned about and fell into despair
at the thought of all my futile labour in this world.
For it can happen that a man works hard,
displaying wisdom, knowledge, and skill,

and yet have to leave his resulting assets
to a man who has not laboured for them at all.
This is not only meaningless, but utterly wrong.

What comes to people for all the hard work and mental stress
    their occupation has forced them to endure in this world?
For all of their days bring pain and grief;
even at night their minds get no rest. This too is futile.
The best that any of us can do
is to eat and drink and enjoy ourselves in our work.
This too, I realised, is from the hand of Nature;
For if it were not for her, who could eat or who could have
    any enjoyment?
To the person who does well in her sight,
Nature gives wisdom, knowledge and happiness,
but to the sinner she gives the task of gathering and amassing
    wealth
only to hand it over to the one who finds favour with her.
But this also is meaningless—a mere chasing after the wind.

Everything has its predestined moment,
every affair on earth its appropriate time.
There's a time to be born and a time to die,
a time to plant and a time to uproot,
a time to kill and a time to heal,
a time to knock down and a time to build up,
a time to cry and a time to laugh,
a time to wail and a time to dance about,
a time to fling stones away and a time to gather them
    together,
a time to embrace and a time to refrain from embracing,
a time to search and a time to leave lost,
a time to keep and a time to throw away,
a time to tear apart and a time to stitch together,
a time to be silent and a time to speak,
a time to love and a time to hate,

a time for war and a time for peace.
Now what does the doer himself stand to gain
from all the hard work he has invested?

I have observed the activities that God has provided
to keep humankind fully occupied.
First, he made everything just right for its own proper time,
and then he put the everlasting universe itself into the human
    mind,
but in such a way that people cannot discover
from beginning to end what it is that God has done.

I have come to realise that nothing is better for people
than to be happy and to do good while they live.
Indeed, it's possible for all people to eat and drink,
and find satisfaction in everything they do.
This is a gift from Nature.
And I believe that whatever Nature produces
will surely endure forever;
for to it nothing can be added,
and from it nothing can be taken away.
Nature has so arranged matters that people may stand in awe
    of it.
Whatever exists has already been,
and what is yet to exist has already been;
for Nature always seeks to repeat the past.

But something more I have seen on the earth:
At the very seat of justice there is wickedness;
in the very place where righteousness should be,
there is transgression.
Therefore this thought came to me:
"Since there's a right time for every affair and every activity,
Nature will bring judgment to both the virtuous and the
    criminal."
So I said to myself,

"The aim of Nature with regard to the human race is to test
   them
and to show them that they are but animals."
For what happens to humans is what happens to animals;
they share the same fate.
As the one dies, so does the other;
the one breath of life is the same for them all.
Humans have no advantage over the animals.
For nothing they do has any lasting significance.
All go to the same place;
all come from dust, and to dust all return.
Who knows whether mankind's breath of life rises upward to
   the heavens
and the animals' breath of life descends downward to the
   earth?
So I saw that there is nothing better for people
than to be happy in their work, because that is their appointed
   lot.
After all, who can enable them to peer into what will happen
after them?

Then I looked again and saw all the oppression
that was taking place on the earth.
See the endless tears of the oppressed
for whom no one provides comfort!
Since their oppressors wield all the power,
no one can ease their suffering.
Therefore I consider the dead (since they have met death
   already)
more fortunate than the living (who are alive to this day).
But more fortunate than both is the one who has never
   existed,
for he has not seen the evil that occurs on the earth.

I saw, then, that all hard work and successful endeavour
spring from a man's rivalry with his neighbour.

This too is futile, like chasing after the wind.

It is said, "The fool folds his arms and destroys himself."

But I say, "Better one handful gained with ease

than two handfuls gained by hard work and chasing after the
wind."

Then I turned back and again saw the futility of this life.

Here is a man all alone:

He has neither son nor brother,

nor can he see any end to his hard work,

and his eyes are never satisfied with his riches.

But he never asks himself, "For whom am I toiling,

and depriving myself of good things?"

This is utterly senseless! What a pitiful state of affairs!

It is said, "Two are better than one,

because they receive a good return for their work."

True enough that if the one fails, the other can help him,

but woe to the one who falls without someone to help him up!

Again, if two lie down together, they will keep warm,

but how can a person keep warm if alone?

And though assailants may overpower one person,

two will be able to withstand them.

A cord of three strands is not easily broken.

It's better to be a poor but wise youth than an old and foolish
king

who can no longer even take care of himself,

even if it's from the prison house the youth has gone forth to
rule

or perhaps was born poor in what was to become his own
kingdom.

I have been observing those who are now living.

They side with the youth who takes the king's place—

and perhaps also would no end of people who lived before
them both—

but as for the generations yet to come, they will find no joy in
    him at all.
So this too—this striving for eminence and acclaim—
is as futile as chasing after the wind.

Watch your step when you go to the house of God.
Being ready to understand is better than offering sacrifice
    with fools
who haven't even the brains to do any real evil.
Be in no hurry to speak,
and do not think of uttering anything hastily before God.
God is in the sky and you are on the earth;
therefore let your words be few.
For just as dreaming results from an abundance of tasks,
so the voice of a fool manifests itself in the abundance of his
words.

When you make a vow to Mother Nature,
do not dally in discharging it,
For she takes no delight in fools.
Therefore perform what you have sworn to do.
It is better for you not to vow at all
than make a promise and not keep it.
Do not allow your mouth
to lead your flesh into sin.
And do not protest to the messenger,
"My vow was a thoughtless mistake."
Why cause Nature to be angry at what you say
and destroy the work of your hands?
If you give free rein to futile dreams
you will only be led to utter empty words.
Remain firmly in awe of Nature.

If you witness social oppression of the poor—
the denial of justice and human rights—
do not be astonished at what goes on.

It's because one bureaucrat is subject to a higher one,
and still higher ones lord it over them both.
And remember that land is of value to everybody,
so every cultivated field has someone ruling over it.
Whoever loves money will never be satisfied by amassing it,
nor the lover of riches with his income.
This shows the futility of seeking wealth.
As fast as a person's goods increase,
so does the number who gather to consume them.
And so what advantage are they to their owner
except for him to feast his eyes on them?
Sweet is the sleep of the worker
whether he eats little or much,
but the feast eaten by the rich man
causes him to toss and turn.

A dreadful evil I have seen on this earth:
hoarded riches that have harmed their owner
or have been lost through a bad investment.
Then he fathers a son
and has nothing in his hand.
As he came forth naked from his mother's womb,
so naked he returns to earth, just as he came.
Not a thing can he retrieve from his labour,
nothing that he can carry away in his hand.
This, then, is another dreadful evil—
that just as a man comes, so he must go.
What does he gain for himself
by having toiled in pursuit of the wind?
He has spent all his days in darkness and mourning,
suffering great anger, sickness and wrath.

Let me tell you what I've come to realise:
It's good and proper simply to eat and drink,
and take satisfaction in all the work

we do on the face of the earth.
After all, this is our human lot
during the limited days of life that Nature gives us.
For to everyone whom Luck has blessed with wealth and
  luxuries,
it has also given the power to enjoy them,
to accept his lot and find enjoyment in his work.
This is a gift from Nature.
But seldom will a person ponder the meaning of his life
when Luck fully occupies him with gladness of heart.

An evil that I have observed in this world,
one that weighs heavily on people, is this:
Luck may give a person such wealth, possessions and honour
that he could wish for nothing more,
and yet take from him the power to enjoy them
and allow a stranger to possess them instead.
This makes no sense; it's a dreadful wrong.

A man may father a hundred children
and live many years;
yet however many be the days of his life
and however elaborate his funeral,
if he cannot enjoy his prosperity,
then, I say, a stillborn child is better off than he.
Though it arrives in futility and departs in darkness
and its name is shrouded in gloom,
though it never saw the sun and knew nothing,
yet it has more rest than does the man,
who lives a thousand years twice over
but gains no benefit from his prosperity.
Do not all go to the same place?

All of a man's efforts are to fill his belly,
yet his appetite is never satisfied.

So what advantage has a wise man over a fool?
What advantage does a poor man gain
by knowing how to deal with life's problems?
It's better to be satisfied with what's in front of you
than to long for distant pleasures—
for that, too, is as futile as chasing after the wind.

Whatever has come to be
was already predestined.
The human condition is already known,
and a person cannot contend against
a power mightier than himself.
The more words he uses,
the more futile it becomes!
So how does that profit anyone?
For that matter, who knows what makes for a good life?
Our days are few and fleeting,
and we are like shadows passing through them.
Who can tell us what will happen
in this world after we are gone?

A good name is better than precious ointment,
and the day of death better than the day of birth.
It's better to go to a house of mourning
than attend a house of feasting,
inasmuch as death is the end of each of us—
a fact that we who are living should take to heart!
Sorrow is better than laughter,
because sadness of countenance matures the mind.
The mind of the wise empathises with the house of mourning,
but the mind of the foolish revels in the house of pleasure.

It is better to heed a wise man's rebuke
than to listen to the praise of fools.
Like the noise of nettles crackling under kettles
is the cackling of fools.

But even the wise man's rebuke may be futile,
for extortion can turn a wise man into a fool,
and a bribe corrupt his mind.

It is better to judge a matter at its end than at its beginning,
and so a patient spirit is better than an arrogant one.
Let not your emotions be quickly aroused,
for anger lurks in the bosom of a fool.
Do not say, "How is it the olden days were better than these?"
For this question does not arise from wisdom.

Wisdom is best when combined with an inheritance
and thus can benefit all on whom the sun shines.
For the protection of wisdom may be like the protection of
    money,
but it has the added advantage of knowing
that wisdom preserves the life of those who possess it.

Consider the works of Nature, and ask yourself
whether anyone can straighten what it has made crooked.
In the days when you prosper, rejoice;
and in the days you suffer adversity, consider this:
Nature is as responsible for the one as for the other,
and manages things in such a way
that we humans have no clue as to how it works.

In these fleeting days of my life I have seen it all,
from a righteous man perishing in spite of his righteousness
to a wicked man living long in spite of his evil-doing.
So do not be over-righteous or try to seem over-wise.
Why make yourself a laughingstock?
Do not be over-wicked and do not prove yourself a fool.
Why die before your time?
Far better that you grasp hold of righteousness
and not lose your grip on wisdom,
for the man who is in awe of Nature will succeed both ways.

It is said, "Wisdom makes the wise man more powerful
than the rulers of the ten cities."
But I say that no human on earth is always in the right,
and does only what is good, and never goes wrong.
So do not pay attention to everything people say,
or you may hear your servant disparage you.
You know in your own heart how many times
you yourself have disparaged others.

I have tested all this by wisdom.
I said, "I am resolved to become wise,"
but I found wisdom was beyond me.
Whatever wisdom may be, it is so distant
and so deep that no one can discover it.
So I shifted my attention to understanding,
to exploring the nature of knowledge and reflection,
so as to be aware of the stupidity of wickedness and the madness
    of folly.

I find more bitter than death the woman who is a snare.
Her heart is a net and her hands are chains.
The person innocent in the sight of God may escape her,
but she will surely capture the sinner.

Look, says the Proclaimer, this is what I have discovered
as step by step I sought to reach a conclusion,
and continued to search without finding it:
I found one upright man in a thousand,
but not one such woman among them all.
The sum and substance of what I have found
is that Nature endows people
with the possibility of leading upright lives,
but they have pursued many harmful devices.

Who can be compared with the wise man?
Who else knows the meaning of things?

A person's wisdom lights up his face
and the grimness of his appearance is transformed.

Obey what the king commands, I say,
on account of your oath of allegiance.
Be in no hurry to leave the king's presence,
nor persist in a cause that displeases him,
for he can do whatever he likes.
Since a king's word is final,
who can say to him, "What are you doing?"
Whoever obeys his command
will experience no harm at all.
A wise mind knows the proper time and procedure.
There is a proper time and procedure for every enterprise,
because of the widespread evil that people do.

Indeed, no one knows the future,
for who can tell what is to come?
No man has control over the breath that gives life,
so no one can decide the day of his death.
As there is no avoidance of battle in time of war,
so wickedness will not save those who are masters of it.
All this I saw for myself
as I applied my mind to everything done on the face of the
    earth,
where people lord it over one another to their own hurt.

Indeed I have seen wrong-doers buried with pomp;
and because they frequented the holy place,
they were praised in the very city where they did their evil deeds.
This also makes no sense.

Wherever judgment for evil deeds is not carried out promptly,
people's minds are filled with ideas of crime,
and a malefactor may commit a hundred crimes and live a
    long life.

Oh yes, I know what they say:
"It will be well for those who fear God,
and show reverence before him;
and it will not be well for the wicked,
for their days will not lengthen like a shadow
simply because they show no reverence before God."
But what occurs here on the earth is absurd.
Some righteous people get what the wicked deserve,
and some wicked people get what the righteous deserve!
This too, I say, makes no sense at all.

Therefore I commend the pursuit of happiness.
There is nothing better for a man to do in this world
than to eat and drink and be happy.
Then joy will accompany him in his work
for all the days of the life Nature has given him in this world.

When I gave my full attention to the study of wisdom,
taking note of all the happenings that occur on earth,
I saw that though a man sleep neither day nor night
in his search to understand all the "works of God,"
he cannot find out what it is that God has done on the earth.
However diligently a man may seek, he will not find out.
Not even the sage who claims to know can find it out.

So to all of this I directed my full attention
seeking an explanation for it all.
People say that the righteous, the wise,
and all their deeds are in God's hands;
but whether things stem from love or hatred,
not a single person will ever know.
Everything they encounter is meaningless
because one Fate comes to everybody—
to the righteous and to the wicked,
to the good, the pure and the unclean,

to those who worship and to those who do not.
As it is with the good man, so it is with the evil-doer;
as with him who swears an oath, so with the one afraid to
    swear.
This is what is wrong with everything that happens in this
    world.
The same fate comes to all.

Moreover, human hearts are full of evil.
There is madness in people's hearts while they live,
and after that they join the dead.
Yet whoever remains in the company of the living has some
    hope;
even a dog, if it is alive, is better off than a dead lion!
For living people at least know that they will die,
while the dead know absolutely nothing.
Nor do they have any hope for further reward,
and even the memory of them is soon lost.
Their loves, their hates and their jealousies have already
    perished.
Never again will they take part in anything that happens on the
face of the earth.

So go and eat your food with gladness,
and drink your wine with a joyful heart,
for Nature has already given approval for you to do this.
Be well dressed for every occasion,
and be presentable in every way.
Enjoy life with a wife you love
through all the days of the fleeting life
that Nature has given you in this world.
And know that this is your reward in life
for the toil and drudgery you have performed in this world.
Everything your hand finds to do, execute with all your might,
for in the underworld of the dead to which you are going

there is no working, no thinking,
no knowledge, and no wisdom.

I have seen something else in this world:
The race is not guaranteed to the swift
nor the battle to the strong;
food does not necessarily come to the wise,
nor wealth to the intelligent,
nor favour to the learned;
for all alike are subject to time and chance.
After all, no person knows when his appointed time will come.
As fish are caught in a cruel net
or birds taken in a snare,
so people can be trapped by a moment of misfortune
that suddenly overtakes them.

But I also saw something else in this world—
an example of wisdom that greatly impressed me.
    Once a small city, with only a few people in it, was attacked
    by a powerful king who surrounded it and built huge
    siegeworks against it. Now it happened that in that city lived
    a poor but wise man, and he could have saved the city by his
    wisdom. Yet nobody remembered that poor man!
Still, I say, "Wisdom is better than strength"
even though the poor man's wisdom was despised
and his words went unheeded.
The quiet words of the wise are more to be heeded
than the ranting of a master of fools.
Wisdom is better than weapons of war.

It takes only one evil-doer to lay waste a mountain of good.
As dead flies make the perfumer's ointment stink,
so a little folly can overpower much wisdom and honour.
The heart of the wise person inclines him to the right,
but the heart of the fool to the left.
Lacking sense, a fool has only to walk along the road

to show everyone what a fool he is.
If the ruler's anger rises against you, do not leave your post;
Steadiness and composure will redeem great offences.

Here is another evil I have seen on the face of the earth:
the sort of error that emanates from the ruler.
Fools are often appointed to high positions
while the rich occupy the lowly ones.
I have seen slaves on horseback,
while princes go on foot like slaves.

He who digs a pit may fall into it;
he who breaks through a wall may be bitten by a snake.
The quarryman may be injured by a stone
or a wood-splitter by a log:
if the wedge is blunt or the axe unsharpened,
he will have to apply excessive force,
but wise foresight will help him to succeed.
If a serpent bites before it is charmed,
there is no value in the charmer's art.
Words from a wise man's mouth win favour,
but the lips of a fool lead to his undoing.
When he first opens his mouth, his words make no sense
and by the end of his speech they become incriminating
    madness,
but still the fool babbles on and on.
Since no one knows what is yet to come,
who can tell him what the future will bring?
A fool's efforts so weary him,
that he doesn't even know his way back to town.

Woe to you, O land,
if you are ruled by an immature youngster
and your princes feast in the morning.
Happy are you, O land,
when your king is of noble birth

and your princes eat at a proper time,
with self-control, and are not drunkards.

Extreme laziness results in the roof caving in,
and leaky homes are a sign of negligence.
Good food leads to laughter, wine makes life merry,
and money is the answer for everything.
Do not make light of the king even in your thoughts,
Nor disparage the rich even in the privacy of your bedroom,
because a bird of the sky may carry away your words;
some winged creature may report what you say.

Cast your bread upon the surface of the waters,
because after many days you will get a return.
Divide it among seven ventures, or even eight,
for you do not know what disaster may come upon the land.
If the clouds are full of rain,
they will empty it upon the earth.
Whether a tree falls to the south or to the north,
it must lie in the place where it falls.
He who keeps watching the wind will never plant,
and he who stares at the clouds will never reap.

Just as you do not understand how life begins,
how it enters the embryo in the womb of a pregnant woman,
so you cannot understand how Nature works
to create everything that exists.

Sow your seed in the morning,
and at evening let not your hands be idle,
for you do not know which undertaking will prosper, this one
    or that,
or whether the two of them will do equally well.

Light is sweet.
It's a joy for the eyes to see the sun.

So if a man lives for many years,
let him rejoice in every one of them.
But let him remember that the days of darkness will be many,
and that everything hereafter is nothingness.

Be happy, young man, while you are young,
and let your heart give you joy in the days of your youth.
Follow the impulses of your heart
and the desires of your eyes,
yet know that for everything you do
Nature will hold you accountable.
Therefore banish anxiety from your heart
and cast off the troubles of your body,
for youth and its early vigour are short-lived.
Therefore think of your grave in the days of your youth,
before the days of trouble come and those years arrive
when you say, "I no longer find any pleasure in life."
Think of it before the sun grows dim,
and with it the daylight and the moon and the stars,
and the clouds return after the rain.
Think of it when the mind starts to wander
and even the strong back begins to stoop,
when the disappearing molars cease to chew
and cataracts dim the eyesight.
Think of it when the doors to the street are closed
and the noise of the grinding mill fades,
when the sound of birds grows faint
and all the daughters of song are humbled.
Think of it when the fear of heights increases
and terrors lurk in the streets,
when the almond tree blossoms
and the grasshopper drags itself along
and desire is no longer stirred.
For humankind goes to its eternal home
and mourners go about the streets.
Think of it before the cord of life is severed,

the golden bowl is crushed,
the jar is shattered at the spring,
and the wheel is broken at the well.
For then the dust returns to the ground it came from,
and the spirit returns to the God who gave it.
"Fast-fleeting," says the Proclaimer. "Impermanent!"
"Everything dissolves into nothingness."

Epilogue
The Proclaimer was not only wise in himself,
But what is more important, he imparted his knowledge to
    the people.
He searched and weighed and set forth a host of parables.
The Proclaimer sought to find just the right words,
and honestly write down what he found to be true.
The words of the wise are like goads.
They are like nails driven firmly home,
by members of a fraternity
and now delivered by one caring guide.
Apart from these, my son, be warned
that there is no end to the making of books,
and much study simply tires us out.
That is the end of the matter, for now you have heard
    everything.
Stand in awe of Nature and do what it requires of you,
for this is the whole duty of humankind.
For everything we do Nature will bring to judgment,
even everything hidden, whether it be good or evil.

12

AFTERWORD

The reason the words of Ecclesiastes seem so relevant to our times can best be understood if we now step back and look at where he stands in the long and complex history of religious thought and cultural change. We in the Western world have long been conditioned to the view that the religious history of humankind was cut in two by the birth, life and death of Jesus Christ. This is because it is from the supposed year of his birth that we in the West number the years of our calendar, both backwards (BC for "before Christ") or forwards (AD for *anno domini,* in the year of the Lord).

But when we survey the whole religious history of humankind from a less biased standpoint, then the more natural though not nearly so clear-cut line of demarcation is what has become known as the Axial Period. This term, coined by the philosopher Karl Jaspers, is increasingly used to refer to the relatively short period of time—a few hundred years on either side of 500 BC—that saw the origin of all the great religious traditions: Zoroastrianism, Buddhism, Jainism, classical Hinduism, Confucianism, Taoism and Judaism (which in turn gave rise to Christianity and Islam).

What knowledge we have of religion prior to the Axial Period leads us to conclude that before the Axial Period no clear distinction could be made between religion and culture. To be sure, most of our primitive ancestors believed the world around them to be inhabited by gods and spirits; but these were all part of the cultural understanding of the world that each ethnic group had slowly accumulated and passed on. Over a period of more than a hundred thousand years, each tribal or ethnic culture had evolved its own way of understanding and responding to the natural environment in which they found themselves living. Because their belief in these gods or spirits was just a part of their cultural knowledge (we could even think of it as a primitive form of "science"), it cannot be accurately called their religion, especially since they had no word for religion in the way we now use that term.

We are able to confirm this conclusion by studying the tribal cultures that survived into modern times untouched by the cultural change that took place at the Axial Period. For example there was no word for "religion" in the language of the Maori, the inhabitants of New Zealand prior to the arrival of Europeans. Their terms "Maoritanga" and "tikanga" refer to the knowledge of what it means to be Maori. This of course includes respect and honour for the gods of Nature, but what was of supreme importance to Maori was simply to absorb their culture from the elders and then nurture and preserve their identity and being as Maori.

What took place during the Axial Period was that major population groups in five or six areas of Asia experienced a radical change in thought that led many to greatly increased levels of critical reflection and individual self-consciousness. It was as if the human race was leaving behind its childhood—which confined people to essentially tribal cultures and required blind obedience to their ethnic inheritance—and entering its adolescent phase by seeking a new kind of human identity that transcended the constraints of tribe and nation. Karen Armstrong has described the Axial Period in considerable detail in her book *The Great Transformation*.

It is illuminating to realise that it was within the Axial Period that Ecclesiastes lived and wrote, and that he was thus engaging in the critical thinking that was a primary characteristic of that time. He was almost contemporaneous with Socrates, Plato, Aristotle and Zeno in Greece; Gautama, Mahavira and the Upanishadic seers in India; and Confucius and Lao Tzu in

China. What we today uncritically regard as pre-Axial religion was in fact undergoing critical review, while what we have long regarded as the great world religions had not yet assumed their defining forms.

Thus Ecclesiastes lived "between the times." As a Jew, he lived during the dawning of the Hellenistic period—aware of both the distant afterglow of the security and optimism of the Davidic kingdom and the long night of conquest and exile—but still centuries before the formulation of rabbinical Judaism, the faith tradition that was to hold the Jewish people together for the next two thousand years. What had been important for the Israelite ancestors of Ecclesiastes was the possession of "the land of promise" and their identity as a people who had a covenantal relationship with their god Yahweh. By the time of Ecclesiastes, however, the Davidic kingdom was no more and its Jewish remnant had become scattered from Babylon to the eastern Mediterranean. The institution of the synagogue, destined to unify the Jewish people and preserve their identity, was as yet only in its embryonic form.

Perhaps this partly explains why Ecclesiastes sounds so pessimistic. He was facing a political and spiritual void. He found nothing to live for and had nothing to look forward to. Even his repeated conclusion—that we can find nothing better to do than to eat, drink and enjoy what we can—was arrived at in a somewhat grudging spirit. Even the God he referred to was no source of comfort, for the "ways of God" were often unjust and in fact were simply a way of speaking about the non-human forces operating in the world. In the end, it made little difference to him whether these were referred to as "the gods" or "God."

What Ecclesiastes had inherited from his cultural past no longer supplied hope for the future or any lasting meaning for the present. Ecclesiastes was not religious in today's popular sense of that term. Even if we define religion very broadly as that which gives some meaning or purpose to life, Ecclesiastes can be said to have had no religion. The philosopher, A. N.

Whitehead, said "religion is what one does with one's solitariness." Ecclesiastes remained a lone individual and found little
to relieve his solitariness. He was forced to reflect on what it
means to be a human individual living in an unfair and uncar-
ing world. Though he searched for wisdom, he found nothing
that would stand the test of time. His study of the world about
him revealed to him no lasting truths that afforded him any
comfort or satisfaction.

So, finding little in life to bring him any comfort, Ecclesiastes
sounds gloomy and pessimistic. The rise of the questioning and
critical thinking that so marked the Axial Period could easily
lead to such a mood. Even the Buddha, in seeking answers to
his quest for meaning, had almost given up the search when
in desperation he took his seat under the bo-tree, where to
his surprise he found Enlightenment. However, failure to find
any meaning or purpose in life can lead to desperation and, in
turn, extreme desperation can lead people to suicide, as alas it
too often does today. Or it can lead to creative solutions, sometimes of a highly appealing nature.

During the Axial Period the analysis of the human situation that perhaps came closest to that of Ecclesiastes was the
Stoic philosophy pioneered by Zeno and later expounded by
the Roman Emperor and philosopher, Marcus Aurelius. And
though it was more positive in its conclusions than those of
Ecclesiastes, and had a wide influence in Rome's classical period, and even left its mark on Christianity, it was too rational
to compete with those that offered more hope and therefore
had a greater emotional appeal.

As it turned out, the Axial Period gave rise to quite a number of religious traditions that captured human imagination.
Even in the Roman Empire, Christianity had to compete with
several close rivals, and these it overcame almost by chance,
for it was political reasons rather than religious conviction
that led Constantine to make it the religion of the Empire. In
the two millennia or more that followed the Axial Period, the
various religious traditions that emerged in Asia may be said

to have served humankind reasonably well insofar as they have given meaning and purpose to people's lives. Jews, Christians, Muslims, Hindus, Buddhists, Confucianists and Taoists found in their respective traditions satisfying answers to the spiritual quest. And many of them still do.

Indeed, by the year 1900, three of these traditions had become so successful and spread so widely that they had virtually divided the globe up among them into the Christian West, the Islamic Middle East and the Buddhist Orient. But by then, some two thousand years after the Axial Period, another worldwide cultural revolution was beginning to emerge. This movement can be initially described as the advent of the modern age; it was marked by an explosion of secular knowledge that resulted primarily from advances in the physical sciences and technology, but also including history, archaeology and the social sciences. This ferment led quickly to the Industrial Revolution, with a consequent population explosion and rapidly increasing urbanization.

I have described in some detail the beginnings and development of the modern age in *Faith's New Age* (republished in the United States as *Christian Faith at the Crossroads*). Some of its seeds are to be found in the philosophy of nominalism, as expounded by the theologian William of Ockham (c 1300–1349). He maintained that it is impossible to provide any cogent proofs of the existence of God and that religious conviction must rest on faith alone and not on reason. At first this challenge was confined to a few brave individuals, but it began to spread through the universities. It precipitated the Renaissance and the Protestant Reformation and finally triumphed in the Enlightenment, whose leading thinkers were labelled the freethinkers.

The Enlightenment really opened the door to the modern age and made the enterprise of empirical science possible. The centuries of Ockham, Copernicus, Galileo, Darwin and Einstein (to name but a few of the pioneers) may be called a Second Axial Period. It has been described as humankind's "coming of age," as if, having entered adolescence in the First Axial Period, the human race is now challenged to enter mature adulthood, standing on its own feet and taking major responsibility for its own future and for that of all life on this planet.

Thus we live in a period that has some similarities to that in which Ecclesiastes lived. All the traditional verities are once again open to question. Nothing is sacrosanct. As the pioneers of the Axial Period questioned the ethnic-based traditions they had inherited, so we are now free to question and critically examine the religious traditions that came out of that period. Indeed, today we are all encouraged to engage in critical thinking and to find our own solutions to the mystery of life. We are continually putting to the test the answers that others both past and present offer us. This is one reason the words of Ecclesiastes from the First Axial Period seem so strangely relevant. They not only manifest the same kind of critical thinking that we engage in today, but they speak to the same basic concerns that challenge us when we do so.

The Western world has now ceased to be the Christendom it once was and is fast losing the overt signs of its Christian past. The great cathedrals of Europe, whose spires once pointed to the heavenly world above and which all Christians aspired to reach, have now largely become inspiring historic monuments, filled not with worshippers but tourists.

Not only has the Second Axial Period shaken traditional Christianity to its foundations, but out of the once vibrant Christian culture that shaped the Western world there has been emerging a new kind of culture that is humanistic, secular and global in its outreach. This secular culture is an indisputable product of Western Christendom, and owes much more to its "Christian matrix" than is usually recognized either by traditional Christians or by the more militant secularists. (This I have argued more fully in *Coming Back to Earth*.)

Only as recently as the nineteenth century did this new, secular culture begin to surface in Europe and to be recognized for what it is. Yet in embryonic form it was already being exported round the globe along with the efforts of the Christian West to Christianise the world. This mission of the church to the world, which took place between the 16th and early 20th centuries, was both driven and made possible by the colonial expansion of Western imperialism.

During the twentieth century, however, the Western Empires disintegrated, the Christian mission to the world ground to a halt, and the non-Christian cultures woke up to what the West had been doing. Christian missionaries were banned in the Islamic world, asked to leave China and continued only as "fellow workers" with other Christians in India. But the global expansion of the West had left a strong deposit of its increasingly secular and humanistic culture, as the cultural revolution of Kemal Ataturk in Turkey bears witness.

To understand the nature of secular culture it may be useful first to describe a secular society or state and then move on to describe secular thought. In a secular society, as opposed to a Christian or Islamic state, citizens are free, both politically and religiously, to make their own choices. Politically, a secular society does not bind its citizens to any ideology, such as capitalism, socialism, or communism. Religiously, a secular society allows its citizens to make their own religious choices. For example, Communist Russia was not truly secular, for it was committed to an atheistic and Marxist ideology; but India (though more overtly religious than Russia) is constitutionally secular in that it is ruled by a democratically elected government that is religiously neutral, leaving its citizens free to be Hindu, Muslim, agnostic, or whatever.

Neither in past Christendom nor in the Islamic world did citizens ever enjoy that degree of religious freedom. Today societies all round the world are becoming more secular (though some much more so than others) in that they are being forced to be more tolerant of diversity in race, religious conviction and sexual orientation. Of course we see many vigorous reactions to this ongoing secularising process. Fundamentalists, whether Christian, Muslim, or Hindu, are strongly opposed to this trend and employ extreme measures in their attempts to turn the clock back. Iran is but one very clear example.

Let's now look at the marks of secular or humanistic thought. First, it abandons the idea of divinely revealed knowledge, or any unchangeable cultural legacy from the past, in favour of empirical observation, which becomes the only source of reliable knowledge. (By "empirical" I mean what we can test for ourselves; by "we" I mean the human species collectively, for the scientific enterprise has expanded into such myriad specialist branches that individuals can no longer do all the testing for themselves. We take much of our knowledge on trust from the experts, the empirical scientists).

Second, secular humanism insists that all humans should be free to think for themselves and to develop their potential for critical and creative thinking. They should not be bound by any set of absolutes handed down from the past, as the Torah has been to the Jew, the Bible to the Christian, and the Qur'an to the Muslim. These cultural resources so highly honoured in the past may now be questioned and critically examined, but at the same time respected as cultural treasures and drawn upon for guidance as individuals may choose.

The third mark of secular thought is the recognition that the physical universe (from vast galaxies to infinitesimal subatomic particles) constitutes all that is. Moreover, this one reality is viewed as a unity, a *uni*verse, and not as consisting of two worlds, one physical and the other spiritual. This does not entail the rejection of human spirituality, for indeed that is what we find expressed in the arts and in all religious endeavour; rather, secular thought acknowledges that all intellectual activity, all emotional experiences and all spiritual aspirations are contingent on the possession of a physical body.

The fourth quality that identifies secular thought is the acceptance of the new knowledge of human origins, gained through anthropology, palaeontology and archaeology—the recognition that planetary life in all of its diversity has evolved from simple to complex forms over a period of some three billion years. We humans are animals who have evolved from pre-hominid mammals and are separated from the other higher animals primarily by the language-based cultures we have slowly and collectively created.

The fifth indicator of secular thought is the acceptance of death as the necessary accompaniment of life—of the fact that humans are mortal creatures like all the other animals and therefore can expect no other domain, spiritual or otherwise, to which we depart when we die.

The sixth ingredient is the realisation that the universe does not exist for any discernible purpose. Even though it operates with various degrees of consistency that we now refer to as the laws of nature, chance is a major component of that operation, and of life itself. We humans have become what we are not by design but by chance, and accident plays an even greater role in our individual lives. If we wish to live purposeful lives, we have to create that purpose for ourselves; in fact, this is what we actually do as we make our many choices in life.

The seventh criterion of secular thought is the recognition that the many different religions by which humans have found meaning in life are all of human origin. They were not revealed by superhuman intelligences but were slowly created as the collective product of tribes and ethnic groups, some of them having been initiated by particularly insightful teachers.

The inescapable fact is that humankind created its various religions specifically to provide meaning or purpose in an otherwise purposeless universe. As soon as humans had reached a sufficiently advanced level of self-consciousness, a sense of purpose became an essential part of the evolutionary mechanism, for it has great survival value. When we have a purpose in life we not only live longer but we live a more satisfying life.

Having sketched the nature of secular thought, we are in a better position to see why the words of Ecclesiastes appear to be so timely. Though unquestionably a product of the First Axial Period, he displayed many of the marks of today's secular thought. Ecclesiastes was a freethinker in the literal sense of that term. He was an early empiricist, basing his convictions not on sacred scriptures or his cultural inheritance, but on his own observations. Although he was somewhat ambivalent about the sky above, he regarded the earth on which he lived as the only lasting reality.

Admittedly, Ecclesiastes showed little sense of history and had no understanding of evolution—but then neither did anyone else until relatively recently. Nonetheless, he fully accepted that we are very like the animals and that we live and die as they do. And like a number of our modern existentialists he found no discernible thread of purpose in the universe or in human existence. Moreover, he acknowledged the significant role of chance in all that happens.

Thus Ecclesiastes displayed a remarkable number of the traits of today's secular person; it is tempting to say that it has taken us twenty-three centuries to catch up to where he was. This paradoxical observation no doubt suggests that despite the great time gap that separates Ecclesiastes from us, it's quite natural that we should arrive at similar conclusions when critical reflection is focused on our shared situation.

Thus the reflections of Ecclesiastes on the human condition led him to an early form of the philosophy of life we today call humanism. This worldview has been spreading, first in the West and then further afield, as part of the secularising process that has resulted from the Second Axial Period. For some in the West it has been a painful experience to learn that we humans are not eternal souls temporarily inhabiting fleshly bodies, but are animals who, in spite of our intelligence and sophistication, remain subject to the bodily limitations of all animal existence.

The essential facts of the human condition are hardly disputable: we are born, we grow, we procreate, we mature and we die. Moreover, the span of a single human lifetime, even if it reaches a century, is but an infinitesimal segment of cosmic time. Much as we might like to live indefinitely, provided we were to keep good health, it is the universe itself that will continue on its way long after we are no longer present to observe it. Even the religions we create and practise in an attempt to give life meaning go through the life stages of birth, growth, change and decay—and whole civilizations have but a limited span of life before giving way to others.

Ecclesiastes enunciated these basic facts of human existence in his own rather blunt and chilling way more than two thousand years ago, and only by a rather ironical quirk of history was his book included in a compendium of holy scriptures and thus preserved. Clearly his thoughts about the human condition left him in a somewhat melancholy state of mind, but need they have the same effect on us? Is it possible that without ignoring or denying these harsh facts of life and death we can today be more hopeful than he appears to have been—even to be joyfully thankful for life? To understand how this can be so, and why many in today's secular world accept his assessment of human existence without succumbing to melancholy, we need now to pursue further a topic raised in the Introduction and occasionally referred to in the Dialogues.

Let me first remind you what I wrote in Chapter Two. As a result of the research undertaken by the Fellows of the Westar Institute (a group of biblical experts commonly known as the Jesus Seminar) it now appears that once we strip away from the historical Jesus the mantle of supernatural divinity with which later tradition clothed him, the recoverable outlines of the human figure who emerges show him to be more of a sage than a prophet, priest, or king. Thus Ecclesiastes was by no means the last of the Jewish sages and not even the most important one. (Those who wish to learn more of Jesus the sage should turn to two books by Robert Funk and the Jesus Seminar: *The Five Gospels: What Did Jesus Really Say?*, and *The Acts of Jesus: What Did Jesus Really Do?*)

These scholars claim to have uncovered what they call the "footprints and the voiceprints" of a "Jesus we never knew" and who was largely hidden from view for nearly two thousand years. Their findings led them to conclude that the historical Jewish figure who sparked off the rise of Christianity was himself a more secular person than has long been thought. At the very time when the edifice of dogmatic Christian doctrine has been crumbling and giving way to secular thought, this has been a timely discovery.

In the view of these scholars, the most genuine traces of what Jesus taught are to be found in his parables and the short aphorisms like those collected in the celebrated Sermon on the Mount. We may be surprised to discover that in the sayings that are undeniably authentic, Jesus never referred to himself at all, never claimed to be the Messiah, never spoke of his coming sufferings and death, and did not predict the end of the world.

Further, in his parables and aphorisms, Jesus said little about God; rather he talked about the *kingdom* of God, often beginning with the words "The kingdom of God is like . . ." and it is pretty clear that by his phrase "kingdom of God" Jesus did not mean the political restoration of the kingdom of David, the age-old dream that such of his contemporaries as the Jewish zealots were ready to fight for. He meant a new kind of human community, a new way of living together in the here and now, one based on mutual love for one another as humans, irrespective of race, class, gender, age. He went so far as to say we should love our enemies.

In his parables, Jesus spoke of everyday things in the lives of his hearers—a robbery on a lonely road, a wayward son, labourers in a vineyard, the baking of bread, the sowing of seed, a lost coin, the growth of a mustard seed, the discovery of hidden treasure, a lost sheep, a dinner party, rich farmers and money held in trust. These were not holy or "religious" topics but very worldly ones. On the basis of his parables and aphorisms it appears that Jesus rarely spoke about religion at all, as that term is commonly understood today.

This has led Don Cupitt, one of today's more radical theologians, to conclude in his recent book, *Jesus and Philosophy*, that "Jesus was an almost secular teacher, whose teaching was entirely concerned with attempting by all means to persuade his hearers to drop everything and commit themselves wholeheartedly to a quite new moral world." This means that if Jesus is to be regarded as the founder of a new religion, then, instead of being named Christianity, that religion should be called "The New Religion of Life."

So the sage Jesus complemented the sage Ecclesiastes in a most important and positive way. On the one hand they both accepted the bare facts of human existence and affirmed that the content and workings of the natural world are but little subject to change. But whereas Ecclesiastes focused on the world's lack of any clear purpose and on the fact that nothing lasts, Jesus fastened on what it is possible to make of life in the here and now while it does last. It can be said that Jesus made a new religion out of the simple but very difficult practice of people serving one another with the aim of creating a new kind of community, the one he called the "kingdom of God."

So whereas Ecclesiastes continued to deplore the shortness of life and its all too frequent injustices, Jesus taught us how to face up to injustices and to overcome them by doing more for others than we need to, by "going the second mile." Jesus set before us a vision of what life can offer when we take the initiative and actively "seek the kingdom of God" by doing good.

Most people are familiar with the now famous words of Martin Luther King, Jr., in which he said he had a dream that all Americans, black and white, would live harmoniously together. If Martin Luther King, Jr., had been like Ecclesiastes he would have despaired of ever seeing any different future for the African-American people, for in his day such an eventuality would have seemed very unlikely, if not impossible. But King was a man strongly influenced by Jesus. He had a dream because Jesus had a dream. Jesus initially told his dream to his own Jewish people when he spoke of the coming of the "reign of God." He was alluding, of course, to the fact that for centuries the Jews had lacked freedom and political independence. But most important of all, the dream Jesus brought was equally applicable to all people, and that is why it inspired Martin Luther King, Jr., as it has countless others.

Whereas Ecclesiastes found no lasting meaning in life, Jesus taught us how to create meaning by learning how to live for others. That is why Dietrich Bonhoeffer came to refer to Jesus not as the Saviour, but as "the man for others." The religion that Jesus founded was not about "life after death"; it was about life *before* death. After all, there can be no going back on the permanent truths about the human condition that Ecclesiastes invoked.

And since the workings of the universe itself appear to lack any hint of purpose, and certainly are not intended to serve us, then what gives meaning to our lives is what we choose to do with them. When we devote our lives to promoting the well-being of others, even to the point of loving our enemies, we give them a meaning that transcends the phenomenon of death itself. It is not because Jesus taught this that makes it important. It was because Jesus' simple but transformative message was able to give life new meaning that he came to be honoured as a teacher. Indeed his followers began to tell stories about him that caused him to be seen as the embodiment of all that he taught. John the Evangelist even put into his mouth the words, "I am the way, the truth and the life." Alas, later generations began to pour such honorifics on Jesus that they lost sight of the radical nature of his teaching, simple though it was. Don Cupitt has gone so far as to say, "By deifying Jesus the Church destroyed almost everything he stood for."

Oddly enough, as the beliefs and rituals of traditional Christianity have been declining, we find that the more permanent deposit it has left behind in secular society is a somewhat less exacting form of the original teaching of Jesus, now often referred to as "Christian values." On close examination, some of these values may prove to be not exclusively Christian at all, and could appropriately be referred to as human values. Such important virtues as honesty, justice, truth and compassion are found in many other cultures also. But the ethical precepts we can trace back to Jesus the sage focus on altruistic behaviour: uncritical charity toward all, doing more than justice requires, unconditional dedication to the welfare of others, and the readiness to love your enemies.

It is all too common for preachers and moralists to deplore the decline of traditional Christianity during the twentieth century and to blame the secularising process for all that is evil and anti-social in the modern world. But we should gratefully remember what has come to fruition in the twentieth century as the result of the motivation provided by the so-called "Christian Values": the slow but gradual spread of democracy, rejection of imperialism, increasing condemnation of war, the rise of a more caring society, affirmation of human rights, increasing acceptance of gender equality, condemnation of racism, protection of personal freedoms, and the as yet incomplete acceptance of sexual diversity.

The values most honoured in the modern secular world owe much to the Christian heritage of the past. All agree that the Christian tradition owes much to its Jewish roots; Paul went so far as to claim it was the fulfilment of the Jewish tradition. In a similar way the secular culture of the modern world originated within, and emerged out of, the Christian culture of the West. It owes much to its Christian matrix.

The Oxford theologian John Macquarrie said in his Gifford lectures, *In Search of Deity*, in 1983,

> There was a time in Western society when "God" was an essential part of everyday vocabulary. . . . But among educated people throughout the world, this kind of God-talk has virtually ceased. . . . People once knew what they meant when they spoke of God, and they spoke of him often. Now the name of God seems to have been retired from our everyday discourse.

In the late 1990s Don Cupitt made a study of our daily speech and discovered what had taken the place of "God" in everyday discourse within the secular world. It is the word "life," or something that implies life. Cupitt found about 150 expressions about life that we English-speaking people in the Western world now commonly use, and many of them have come into use only in the last few decades. Here are a few of them: "Get a life." "You only live once." "Get on with life." "Take life as it comes." "Lust for life." "That's life!" "This is the Life." "Such is Life!" And whereas on taking leave of someone we often used to say, "God bless!" now we say, "Have a good day!"

Ecclesiastes and Jesus were two Jewish sages who thought deeply about life. Ecclesiastes was right to insist that we must face up to the reality of the human condition and to be ever mindful of the finiteness of life. Alas, he was so overcome by the sense of its futility that at times he even came to hate life. The best he could offer were such injunctions as: "Enjoy life with a wife you love through all the days of the fleeting life that Nature has given you in this world" and "Eat and drink and enjoy yourself in your work."

Jesus never contradicted the basic facts of life and death that Ecclesiastes had so clearly stated, but he taught us to look beyond ourselves and to care for others. Jesus had an understanding of the essential importance of communal living that Ecclesiastes lacked—perhaps because of his exalted social status and individualistic concerns. Jesus sketched a vision of a human community in which prejudice, friction and enmity would be overcome by love. In the twenty-first century humanity must either take the necessary steps to become a mutually caring global community or bring about its own demise. As we face the coming worldwide crises, little could be more relevant than the words of these two Jewish sages, Ecclesiastes and Jesus of Nazareth.

BIBLIOGRAPHY

Karen Armstrong. *The Great Transformation*. Atlantic Books, 2006.

Don Cupitt. *Jesus and Philosophy*. SCM Press, 2009.

——. *The New Religion of Life in Everyday Speech*. SCM Press, 1999.

Charles Darwin. *On the Origin of Species*, first published in 1859.

Paul Davies. *The Mind of God*. Penguin Books, 1992.

Robert Funk and the Jesus Seminar. *The Acts of Jesus: What Did Jesus Really Do?* HarperSanFrancisco, 1998.

— *The Five Gospels: What Did Jesus Really Say?* Macmillan, 1993.

Lloyd Geering. *Christian Faith at the Crossroads, a map of modern religious history*. Revised edition. Polebridge Press, 2001. Originally published as *Faith's New Age*. Collins, 1980.

——. *Tomorrow's God: How we Make our Worlds*. Polebridge Press, 2000. Originally published by Bridget Williams Books, 1994.

——. *Christianity without God*. Polebridge Press, 2002.

——. *Coming back to Earth: From gods to God to Gaia*. Polebridge Press, 2009.

John Macquarrie. *In Search of Deity*. SCM Press, 1984.

Jacques Monod. *Chance and Necessity*. Collins, 1972.

Richard L Rubenstein. *After Auschwitz*. The Bobbs-Merrill Co, Inc, 1966.

INDEX

ABOUT THE AUTHOR

Sir Lloyd Geering, ONZ, GNZM, CBE, is a public figure of considerable renown in New Zealand where he is in constant demand as a lecturer and as a commentator on religion and related matters on both television and radio. He is the lecturer for St. Andrew's Trust for the Study of Religion and Society, and Emeritus Professor of Religious Studies at Victoria University of Wellington, New Zealand.

Appointed to the Order of New Zealand in 2006, Geering was previously honored as *Principal Companion of the New Zealand Order of Merit* in 2001 and as a *Companion of the British Empire* in 1988. He is the author of several books including *Christianity without God* (2002), the precursor to *Coming Back to Earth,* and a trilogy of books—*Christian Faith at the Crossroads* (revised 2001), *Tomorrow's God: How We Create our Worlds* (reprint 2000), and *The World to Come: From Christian Past to Global Future* (1999).

In 1966, Geering published an article on "The Resurrection of Jesus" and, in 1967, another on "The Immortality of the Soul," which together sparked a two-year public, theological controversy that culminated in charges by the Presbyterian Church of New Zealand—of which he is an ordained minister—of doctrinal error and disturbing the peace of the church. After a dramatic, two-day televised trial, the Assembly judged that no doctrinal error had been proved, dismissed the charges and declared the case closed.

A documentary about the Lloyd Geering, entitled *The Last Western Heretic,* was broadcast on TVNZ in January 2008. It can be seen in its entirety on YouTube.

LaVergne, TN USA
19 July 2010
190123LV00001B/3/P